Feed the
GOAT

Feed the GOAT

Shaun Goater

with David Clayton

SUTTON PUBLISHING

First published in 2006 by
Sutton Publishing Limited · Phoenix Mill
Thrupp · Stroud · Gloucestershire · GL5 2BU

Reprinted 2006 (twice), 2007

British Library Cataloguing in Publication Data
A catalogue record for this book is available from the British Library.

ISBN 978-0-7509-4502-8

Typeset in 11½/16 pt Sabon.
Typesetting and origination by
Sutton Publishing Limited.
Printed and bound in England by
J.H. Haynes & Co. Ltd, Sparkford.

*This book is dedicated to my grandmother,
the late Dorothy Dillon.
She saw the beginning, the middle and
I wish she could have been here to see
the end of my career.
Rest in Peace, Momma.*

Contents

Acknowledgements

When I was first asked by my publisher to put my auto-biography together my thoughts went to the ups and downs of my career, from the early days playing at the Desert Field in Bermuda, to the Wembley Finals and derby games at Maine Road and Old Trafford. I am proud of my achievements and the desire and strength of mind it has required along the way. One thing is for certain, you cannot succeed in any industry without the love, support and guidance of people along the way.

First and foremost I would like to say thank you to my mother, Lynette Goater, for her love and support from, as she tells me, the age of two, telling me I would be a great footballer. Thanks are due to many others, too.

To my grandmother, the late Dorothy Dillon, who was the rock of the Goater family and who said to me, 'Whatever the future holds, always stay humble as the Lord can take it all away', words I have never forgotten. To my sister, Juanita, who is always supportive, even though she doesn't like football!

To Russell Calvin Smith, my stepfather, for his continual support through my career. To my extended Goater family for always wishing me well and being there.

To Andrew Bascome, who has been my inspiration, mentor and a father figure to me. To the late Bernice Bascome and her grandsons and my good friends Herbie Jr and David Bascome for making their home feel like mine when I needed it.

Harold 'Dock' Dowling, Leroy 'Poker' Augustus and Woolly Wendall Baxter – youth coaches at North Village – thank you for all your advice and knowledge in the earlier years.

To the Bermuda Football Association for their continual support over the years.

To Mark Trott for writing that letter to Manchester United FC.

Thank you Joe Royle, for giving me the opportunity at a wonderful club, for having belief in my abilities and in me, and for providing the foreword to this book.

To Willie Donachie, who was instrumental in improving my game.

To Paul Connor, my sports physiologist, who helped me through the tough times at Manchester City – you taught me how to be mentally stronger when I most needed it.

To Billy McEwan for giving me a second chance at being a professional footballer and for giving me the chance to learn about English football.

To John Ward, former manager of Bristol City, who was a great man-manager, and the man who knew how to get the best out of me.

Many thanks to Terry Connor for making strikers' shooting sessions insightful and fun at Bristol City.

To Steve Tilson and Paul Brush, who convinced me to play one final year with Southend and for allowing me to be myself and play with the energy and enthusiasm I naturally carry with me.

Thank you to all the fans at all the clubs I represented, but especially the Manchester City fans for their love and unbelievable support – they have given me many precious moments through the years and, trust me, I'm City till I die!

To David Clayton for never giving up trying to persuade me to write this book and for turning my voice into written words.

Thanks to Paul Dickov for helping me turn around my career at City – that boy has the heart of a lion and I'm delighted to see him back at City again.

To Lawrence Trott for encapsulating my thoughts and views so succinctly over the years he interviewed me for the *Royal Gazette*. He wrote things the way I wanted them to be and there was never an agenda with him – and for that I'm eternally grateful.

To my agent, friend and mentor Mark Georgevic for all the good advice through the years and to his family for understanding the long hours we sometimes spent on the phone.

To my mate, Kyle Lightbourne, who motivated me through our personal goal scoring battles while in the lower divisions and to his wife Rosemarie, who has been a good friend of my wife and me through the years.

Finally, to my wife, Anita, and my daughters Amaya and Anais – thank you for your loving support through all the ups and downs of my career over the years and for assuring me that love at home is unconditional.

Shaun Goater
June 2006

Foreword

I first saw Shaun Goater play in 1990 when Rotherham United reserves mauled my Oldham Athletic reserve side on the sloping pitch at Millmoor. I made a mental note to keep an eye on the gangly striker up front, who was chasing every lost cause and generally out-battling our back four. I could not help but be impressed by his honesty and willingness to go in where it hurts. I would, however, admit that at this stage there was no great hint as to the future goal machine that Leonardo Shaun Goater would become – in fact it took him five seasons to get into double figures as a scorer. But once he started he never stopped.

The next step for Shaun took him to one of my old clubs, Bristol City. The £175,000 that they invested in him will count as one of the best pieces of business they ever did. I always kept in touch with Shaun's progress through an old friend from my playing days at Bristol, Chris Garland. Every other week Chris would ring and tell me of Shaun's progress and the scoring charts confirmed what I was being told.

Deadline day in 1997 saw me as the new manager at Manchester City, desperately looking for a goalscorer to keep the ailing Sky Blues in the First Division. Shaun came to mind and after protracted negotiations we signed the likeable Bermudian for £400,000 – as good a £400,000 as I have ever spent.

I went to dinner in Manchester the night before signing Shaun and bumped into Sir Alex Ferguson. I told Sir Alex of my intention of signing Shaun, who had been released by Manchester United as a young man. The soccer peer was unequivocal in his praise and tipped Shaun to be a big success. He was right!

Shaun carried on scoring of course, and three goals in seven games confirmed that his scoring touch had not deserted him. However, he had not arrived in time to save us from the drop.

It is no secret that Shaun's all-action galloping style was not instantly endearing to the Maine Road faithful, bred on a diet of Rodney Marsh, Colin Bell, Francis Lee *et al.*, but the best fans in the business always loved a trier, and boy, was Shaun a trier!

The following two campaigns were promotion seasons and the doubters were dispelled as the natural charm and honesty on and off the pitch led to the chant 'Feed the Goat and he will score', and score he did, at the prodigious rate of just under a goal every two games.

I often tell my players that one of the best feelings in life is to prove people wrong. These early doubters of Shaun must cringe when reminded of his status now as a Manchester City legend.

Those who met Shaun at supporters' clubs all over Lancashire have been charmed by the natural smile and honesty of the big Bermudian.

I know that Shaun finished his career down at Southend recently. They too have come to love 'The Goat', and it is no coincidence that, in his only season at Roots Hall, they won promotion.

A career that started slowly and climaxed at Manchester City means that Shaun will never be forgotten when goalscorers are talked about. Well done Shaun, and thank you from just one of your grateful managers. I wish you, Anita and your children all the best back on your beautiful island; I am sure that another successful career awaits you there. 'The Goat' for Prime Minister? Don't bet against it!

Joe Royle
May 2006

CHAPTER ONE

The Pond Dog

Far from the idyllic images of white sand and aqua-coloured waters, my earliest memories of growing up in Bermuda are a million miles from the picture-postcard images most people have of my home island. Following the assassination of the Bermudian governor Richard Sharples in 1973, there were large-scale riots in and around my home town of Hamilton, the capital, and as mobs wandered the streets smashing windows and torching public buildings, a four-year-old Leonardo Shaun Goater was smack bang in the middle of the unrest, excited by all the commotion though not actually involved.

So for all those who imagined my early days were spent lying on a beach with a fishing rod in one hand and a cool drink in the other, think again – and there was no affluent sea-front home for the Goater family, either. We lived on Court Street, right in the heart of the ghetto, next to the Spinning Wheel nightclub, which is still going strong today. We had a yard, but in truth the whole of Court Street was my yard – I knew everyone and everything on my little bit of turf, and though it probably stretched no more than a few hundred yards in either direction, it was my world and I loved it.

During the riots many roads were blocked by burned-out wrecks and cars sped past our house at all hours, often loaded with planks of wood, bricks and anything else that could be used to cause damage. I even saw the odd machete – but thankfully no guns – and even an impressionable young kid like me could see that the guys were intent on causing some serious damage. There was one occasion I remember vividly because I had strayed too close to the action and was affected by a tear-gas canister fired by the police. My eyes were stinging and I couldn't see a thing, and although I could hear my mum shouting to me from down the street, I thought, 'Yeah, but what are these guys up to and what are they going to do next?'

At that age it's all a game, but the neighbourhood guys were always looking out for me and they knew where to draw the line. If I was too near danger, they'd turn around and say 'Shaun, it's time to go home – you need to go now', and mostly I followed their advice – mostly! Even the so-called bad guys knew that kids needed to be kept away from anything underhand, and they made sure you were ushered away if you got too close. Maybe that was the big difference between then and now. Right up to the age of 12 all the other kids I knew who grew up with me were kept out of harm's way as much as possible.

My granny – Dorothy Dillon – was a popular and respected figure in our neighbourhood and I believe that's why the older guys used to make sure I didn't become involved in anything I shouldn't. I think they knew that if I had come to any harm they would have had to answer first to her, and then to my mum, and then to my aunts – and only a fool would risk the wrath of those ladies! People who were probably into drugs, stealing and other types of activities the police would have been interested in knew where to draw the line, and so, while I may have witnessed things most kids of that age would not normally have seen, it was always from a distance. If anyone did try to sell weed in the alley that ran down the side of Granny's house she'd be out in a flash to tell them in no uncertain terms what she'd do if they didn't take a walk, and I can assure you they walked away every time and didn't try again.

My granny was a large, heavy-set lady and was in her mid-forties around the time of the unrest, and she was also at the height of her powers. When she raised her voice everyone listened – and she could make the house rattle if she was aiming a verbal volley at somebody. The house where I lived in Court Street was hers, and along with my mum, Lynette Goater, there was my aunt Idae Mae and another of my mum's sisters, known as Mama Julie. I also had cousins who lived there or stayed a short while, and at times it was hard to keep track of who was stopping over and who was living there, but I loved it because it was always a happy place to be, and exciting. The house was the centre of the Goater family's world; friends and neighbours would stop by, or if it was late, family members would sleep over.

It was also a place where relatives stayed when they were trying to get on their feet. When their fortunes improved they'd move out and find their own home. My mum and I moved in and out a couple of times over the years, but no matter where we went my granny's house was always there for us and felt like home. I remember the fantastic parties she used to hold there, too. There were so many people there you'd have thought they were block parties. She would sometimes ask me to dance in the middle of the room and I and my cousins, who had one or two fancy moves up our sleeves, lapped it up. The parties would go on into the early hours of the morning and for me, aged five or six, it was normal to stay up, trying to join in the fun. Of course my mum or aunts would tell me it was time to go to bed and I'd say, 'Yeah, yeah, I'm going up now', before sneaking back into the midst of everything.

There was no time to watch TV back then, because there was always something going on – that is, unless my mum and granny were watching the late afternoon American soaps. Man, they didn't budge until those shows were over – and some of them seemed to go on for ever!

During the day it seemed as though the whole neighbourhood would stop by to say 'Hello' and have a chat, and of course everybody knew me because I was 'connected' to the Godmother! In fact, I believe the only difference between Don Corleone and my granny was that if she had ordered a professional hit it would have been with a well-aimed slipper, rather than with a revolver.

Financially my mum and I didn't have much, and I suppose we were a working-class family, but I have nothing but happy memories of those days on Court Street. When we moved out for the first time it was only a couple of blocks, to an area known as Happy Valley.

At this point you may be wondering why I've not mentioned my dad, and the answer is fairly simple: he was not around, and it would be almost twenty years before I knew for sure who he was. He is not even mentioned on my birth certificate and from the day I was born my mum raised me on her own. She was 22 when she had me, and all through my early years I lived with my mum, granny, aunts and cousins. Not knowing or seeing my dad was not a big deal for me because I'd never known anything different. I never asked my mum 'Who is my daddy?' because all my cousins were in the same boat, none of their dads was around, it was perfectly normal and there was no stigma at all. I was not down and out, I was healthy, I had food and clothes and I was happy with my lot. I was okay, and if my dad was not around, so what? That's how I felt, and I can't say I have changed right up to this day. Certainly I didn't get everything I ever wanted, but everything I ever needed – like football boots, or my first bike – I got. Sometimes I would say to my mum, 'Hey, I want that', or 'I really need this', and she would reply, 'No, no, no, you don't really need it and you ain't getting it, I can't afford it', and I would get over it. But she always found the money for the things that she knew would enrich my life or help me develop.

My mum worked around the clock to bring in enough money for us to live a comfortable life. Her main job was at the Bermudiana Hotel in Hamilton. Many of my family used to work in the hotel trade, often as housemaids. I could turn up at my mum's place of work and the chances were that I would see someone I knew or was related to, so tracking her down was never a problem. My aunts Pam, Julie and Maxine and my uncle Clyde always seemed to be working at the same place as my mum – it was definitely a family business. Mum was always a popular figure, because apart from being a good-hearted and happy woman, she was a mean pool player, and also a good footballer! She was as competitive a person as you are ever likely to meet and in later years her first words during a transatlantic phone call would be, 'Did you win?' So you could say the secret of my success can be traced back to my mum and her career with the Bermudian Cosmos – named after their idols, the New York Cosmos, whom mum watched on TV whenever she had the chance.

I was playing football myself by this time and spent a lot of time with the Caisey brothers, Albert and Clinton. Albert was one of the best left-backs of his day and on a typical afternoon we would chill out at their house and then go and play football for a few hours on the nearby field. We'd play various skills games – one-touch, two-touch or keep-ups – and cricket until the sun went down.

Mum often worked two shifts at the Bermudiana Hotel – one during the day and another in the evening, as a waitress. She worked there for fifteen or twenty years, pretty much all through my formative years, in fact. If she worked late, I'd stay at my granny's – where else?

When I was around 9 years old we moved out to West Pembroke, about a five-minute car ride from Court Street but still considered 'town' – and a real journey for Bermudians when you consider the island's size! We moved to Marsh Folly when I was about 10 and again mum would work late. As I got a little older I'd be on my own, sometimes until about ten o'clock at night, but I'd stay up until she came home because she would bring back something nice for me to eat – steak or fish from the hotel – and it was a treat I looked forward to. She always cooked something for me to eat before she went to work, but I would always save room for the hotel food and I'd say, 'Yeah, that's fine and I'll eat it, but bring me home some steak, mama!' I told my friends, 'Yeah, my mama can cook really well – we eat steak every night!'

Living in Marsh Folly had a major impact on my life because it was here that I became good friends with Andrew Bascome, who would eventually, in my opinion, become Bermuda's best footballer. He became my mentor and, in many ways, a father-figure, even though he was only about six years older than me. I first met Andrew at West Pembroke as I walked to Victor Scott primary school. I had been kicking a tin along the street, doing the odd step-over here and there, and I had seen Andrew a couple of times on the journey when, one morning, he came over and said, 'Come on then kid, what have you got for me?' urging me to take him on with the tin can. I took up the challenge, and started to look forward to our daily little battles. When we moved to Marsh Folly we discovered that the Bascome family lived virtually next door – and I suppose you could argue that destiny was already edging me down a particular path. I soon became close friends with Andrew and his brothers, Herbie Jr and David, and I suppose it was my good fortune that they were all talented footballers.

David was closer to me in age so we soon became good friends and from the age of about 11 we became best mates. By this point I was immersed in football, as well as cricket, and I was determined to show Andrew and his brothers what I was made of. I might not have had any blood brothers of my own, but these guys felt like family, and in retrospect the Bascome brothers were crucial to my future in the game. They loved football and cricket, and there was always an enjoyable edge to our knockabouts on the field. I still saw my old friends from Court Street from time to time, but I was now immersed in football and as time went on I saw my old buddies less and less.

David had been brought up by his granny and was more disciplined than many kids of his age – including me. He had to do his household chores before he could play out on the field, and if we were out there playing football five days out of seven David would be at home for maybe two days doing chores for his granny. As for me, I played every day and you couldn't have kept me away if you had tried.

I remember that one day I asked David's granny if it would be okay to sleep over and she said, 'Of course'. My mum was happy with that, but then it was only three doors away. From then on I stayed over a lot, just hanging out with the boys, playing football and cricket. Sometimes we would go down and play with the Caisey brothers, but if David's mum said he couldn't we would knock the ball around his yard.

We would go and watch David's brothers playing for local league side North Village. They were in the junior team; Andrew was in a class of his own, while Herbie was a fair player, too. Andrew was an intelligent boy and attended one of the best schools in Bermuda. He would tell David things such as 'Remember who you are and who you represent; don't go out without combing your hair; tuck your shirt in; make sure your shoes are clean'. He was a parental figure for David, and as I got older he became more of a father-figure in my life, too. He not only influenced my football but helped shape me into the man I am today. He was a perfect role-model for any young boy.

When his young brother Herbie grew his hair into dreads, Andrew would say, 'You don't want to be having dreads, it looks untidy – come on, comb your hair'; but funnily enough in later years Andrew grew his hair into dreads too, and with that hairstyle comes a lot of baggage, in that people perceive you to be a certain type, and think, 'Oh, he must smoke weed and do this or that'. I only know the role-model who was there for me when I needed a little guidance, and that's the Andrew I always think of.

Back home my mum had started seeing a guy called Russell Calvin Smith, and a few years later he fathered a little girl, my sister Juanita. I was a teenager when she arrived but I could not have been prouder to have a baby sister, and I decided I would be big brother and, when needed, father-figure and mentor for her. If my baby sister needed me I was always there because I never saw it as a chore. After a couple of years we were on the move again, this time to Warwick. Mum still had to work. On Sundays she was out for as much as three hours and I would do my share of babysitting.

I was around 14 at this point, and I always made sure that I went out and played football into the early evening. I was an independent kid and, as much as I was still a mama's boy, I was happy to take care of myself and hang out with my friends. If it wasn't sport of one kind or another I would be out skateboarding or on my bike. I was a mean skateboarder and we skated down Pond Hill at speed and did jumps off small hills. Being 'Pond Dogs' – the slang term for people who lived or were raised in the area around the city dump known to one and all as 'the Pond' – my friends and I couldn't always afford to buy BMXs, Mobylettes or the other popular bikes of the day, so made our own from spare parts we found at the dump – chains, seats and wheels, anything we could adapt into a racing machine. People would throw away some amazing stuff and there were always plenty of bits lying around – and the bikes we made were fast, too.

Sometimes we would use a Chopper wheel at the front and a Mobilette wheel – a big, heavy motorbike wheel – at the back, and that made the bike better for racing down hills. We would reach fair speeds and had guys at the bottom of the hill stopping traffic so that we had a clear, safe run – it also helped having no brakes to call upon! We didn't see any danger in it and we held challenges between kids from different areas, racing on different tracks and representing our street or village. We literally lived by the seat of our pants and were into everything, although we never progressed beyond the mischievous. If we wanted to go fishing down by the harbour we would jump over the bakery wall, grab a tray of stale bread that was waiting to be thrown away, and then go fishing at places where we had seen schools of fish – snappers and bream. They would swim in front of the ships docked at Hamilton Harbour, in water illuminated to a depth of 100ft by the ships' lights. We would drop our lines down, and despite the fish being so big I couldn't catch a bloody thing, yet my friends could catch anything.

That, along with swimming and the occasional cliff diving over at North Shore and the Ducking Stool, was what the majority of kids did in Bermuda, and although our geographical surroundings were undoubtedly beautiful they made no real impression on us because that was all we had ever known. The sun shone constantly, the sea was blue and crystal clear, and it was our home. We used to see the big liners dock in the harbour and unload wealthy tourists in their hundreds. The wealth gauge for the locals was that if you shopped on Front Street you had money. I recall that my mum took me out to dinner one time at Elbow Beach Hotel, an affluent hotel out on Bermuda's south shore and I wore my school uniform in order to look smart, so you can probably guess that we never shopped on Front Street.

Tourists are part of life on the island and I can remember leaning on the harbour wall on one occasion, staring up at a huge ship and thinking, 'Yeah, I'd like to cruise over to New York on that one day'. Then I could shout down at the people and say 'Hey! I'm up here, see you in a few weeks, I'm off to New York City!' The visitors were good for Bermuda's economy and they were the reason many locals had jobs. When my mum did waitress work in the evenings, it was the tips of affluent Americans that helped boost her wages. I just hoped one day I could help her.

I suppose there is one thing I should touch upon before closing this chapter, because it is something Bermudians are constantly asked about – the Bermuda Triangle. So far as the islanders are concerned it just doesn't exist. My granny went to America once or twice and she used to tell me, 'Well, I'm still here and I flew right through it'. If you asked the locals about the Triangle they'd just say, 'You got here okay, didn't you?' The mystery for which my home is perhaps most famed only seems to fascinate people outside Bermuda.

CHAPTER TWO

Opportunity Knocks

U ntil I moved to England I had hardly heard of Clyde Best.
Best was one of the first black players really to make an
impression in English football, and he became a popular
figure for West Ham United in the early 1970s. You would think
that Bermuda's first really successful football export would be a
legendary figure and a household name back home, but that was
not the case at all.

There were stars who played for various Bermudian league
clubs, and I knew who they were. For instance, I knew the big
names who played for Somerset – Clyde Best's team when he was
based on the island, though this was a few years after he'd left for
England. Watching Andrew Bascome play regularly for North
Village, I learned who the really talented players were – the guys
who turned on the style for the First Division clubs and also
represented Bermuda at international level. Yet I wasn't aware of
our most successful export until I came to England. People would

say, 'You *must* know Clyde Best', and they were taken aback when I replied, 'Who is Clyde Best?' The reason was partly to do with the lack of media coverage at the time, but also because he never came home until the late 1990s.

When he left England he moved to America and it was only later, around 1997, that he came home, but by that point I had been in England for eight years and both Kyle Lightbourne and my best mate David Bascome, who was playing in the indoor league for Harrisburg Heat, were also doing well, so the focus and attention he might have received had shifted onto us. He managed to get some kids out on community programmes, but this was more likely because their parents knew who he was and what he had done in the past, and the fact remained that he was more famous in England than in Bermuda.

My early football heroes were Andrew Bascome, Ralph 'Gumbo' Bean, Woolly Baxter, Joe Trott, and Parks and Punchie Dill. These were the North Village stars, and they were entertainers. It was a great era for Bermudian football and I was really lucky to be around at a time when my own career was just beginning to show promise. Had Andrew not been a mentor for me I would have had another seven to choose from, because North Village was blessed with great players.

This was a time when Bermuda would easily beat the USA in international matches, as well as many of the Caribbean sides. Footballers from the island played for teams such as New York Cosmos. Sam Neusun was a goalkeeper who played in the same team as Pele, and he incurred the great man's wrath by holding on to the ball too long. 'He can't play in goal,' Pele had said, 'he needs to give the ball to us!'

All young players had mentors in that golden era of Bermudian football, whether they played for St George's, Somerset or North Village – Kyle Lightbourne had a mentor, Marichal 'Mop' Astwood, at Pembroke Hamilton Club (PHC), a team based in Warwick. It wasn't hard to find a role-model back then, and I would play for the North Village minors and then for the bantams on a Saturday morning. Then, if the junior team only had a dozen players, I might get a place on the subs' bench and that was a real privilege – mixing with the big boys!

I would watch Andrew and Herbie Bascome play for the juniors; Andrew was easily good enough to play professionally. But at that time, even to suggest leaving Bermuda was considered nothing short of certifiable. People would say, 'What? You're *leaving* Bermuda and going into the big world? You must be crazy.' I think that was enough to deter Andrew from pursuing his career overseas. He could have signed for a professional club in Mexico, but if he had gone I think he would have been homesick. He was the best talent of his age without a doubt.

There was no national stadium as such in those days, and Bermuda played on a field with a large hill at one side, packed with spectators – maybe up to 7,000 on certain occasions, not bad for a country with only 60,000 inhabitants. North Village would average around 1,500 fans, although nowadays you would be lucky to have 200 people watching, because interest has waned and the league needs a bit of a shake-up.

I began my association with North Village at the age of 8 and the coach at the time, Harold 'Dock' Dowling, would say to me, 'Done your homework yet, Shaun?' and even if I said 'Yes', he would say, 'I can tell you haven't just by the way you answered – go home and do your homework', and he would send us away until he was certain we had. He was a tough disciplinarian and I would be sick if I missed training, but he was just doing the right thing. When we trained my friends and I would stay and play football until everyone else had gone home and it would be David Bascome, the Caisey brothers and me turning off the lights at the end. We would practise different tricks, one-on-ones and anything we could do, to improve our game, just because we loved playing so much. The coach would shout, 'Okay you guys, pack up, it's time to go', and we would tell him we'd switch everything off and jump the fence to get out. He would smile, shake his head and lock up.

We trained at a field known as the Desert, right next to the Pond – in fact the Desert is now part of the city dump. It was dry and bobbly, but to us it was a field of dreams because we knew the bounces, slopes and other anomalies. In later years I would look at its brutal surface and wonder how I ever managed to play on it at all. Maybe my knack for scoring from anywhere in the box with any part of my anatomy developed because I looked for the unpredictable and had learned how to deal with it – and that is how the legend of the 'Goater clean strike' was born!

One of my earliest memories as a player is of representing my school team and my mum standing on the sidelines shouting, 'Give the ball to my son! He'll win the game for you – give it to Shaun!' I asked her to be a little more discreet ('Mama, please be quiet!') but I think I scored four goals in that game, and she was unrepentant, saying, 'See, just give the ball to my son and he'll score'. Perhaps this was an early version of 'Feed the Goat'?

In later years, when I was around 15, I wanted to play in North Village's first team but was not allowed to because of my age, so I took part in what we called backyard kicks when there was no training scheduled. These free-for-alls took place at Bernard's Park, which is another field adjacent to the Pond and pretty well anybody could take part in these games; if you wanted, you could pull your car over and just join in a game of shirts and skins with players of all ages, although at that time they were mostly older than me. There were four main characters that stood out in these kick-abouts, including a guy known as Geese, but to us he was like Maradona – tricky and skilful. Ting was a no-nonsense tough guy who would come in hard, leave you crumpled on the ground, and then tell you to get on with it! Funnily enough, nobody ever called a foul against him, and if they did it was usually just as they were about to drive off in their car! Then there was Shaggy Dog, Bermuda's best long-range passer. He would give a pass and shout 'Sorry for giving you such a great ball'. Wire was another character, a self-appointed referee and commentator, though not the best player in the world. I played in these scrimmages, which were mainly between squad members from North Village, Boulevard and Devonshire Cougars, and I thought, 'Yeah, there's no fear for me here'. I was holding my own and people would say, 'You're ready, you know? You could play for the first team now.' I wanted to play for the junior team before my time, but coach Woolly Baxter would not allow it, so I went to play for Boulevard – a team full of dreads! Their pre-match preparation was to put on a bit of Bob Marley and they had other, 'medicinal', ways of relaxing before the games, too! But they let me play for their junior team and I stayed with them for a year; I had needed to up the stakes and play against older opponents and Boulevard gave me the chance to do exactly that. I found an outlet with, shall we say, a more relaxed attitude to the laws of the game (and certain other laws too!).

I didn't play every week because they too had a talented side, but I believe I featured in about half of their matches, in midfield, and my game then was mainly about creating chances for others. After a year I returned to North Village, and this time they allowed me to play for the junior team. Obviously they thought I was ready now – either that, or they just wanted me back among their ranks.

It was around this time that I met the girl who would eventually become Mrs Goater. I remember seeing Anita – the object of my affections – at school when I was about 16 and in the fourth year, and I said to my mate Sean Dill, 'I like her! Yeah, I *really* like her'; so, thanks to the tried and tested communication link of Chinese whispers, she eventually found out she had an admirer. I was always saying 'Hi' to her and absently smiling at her, and occasionally I would go to her class and tell her teacher that the principal wanted to see Anita. When she came into the hallway she would say, 'What does the principal want to see me for?' and I'd say, 'He doesn't want to see you, girl, it's me that wants to see you!' She would ask me if I was serious and then head towards the principal's office, leaving me thinking, 'He doesn't want you – only me'. I'd gone from a Pond Dog to a hound dog in my pursuit of her affections.

I think she realised just how much I thought of her when she went home on her moped one lunchtime and didn't return to school for the afternoon classes. I waited around where she usually parked her moped and after a while I knew something was wrong. I asked her friends where she was and eventually discovered a car had pulled out on her and knocked her off her machine. I set off for her house as soon as I finished school – by this time she lived only a ten-minute walk from my house. I went to her room and there she was, looking sorry for herself and a little sore and bedraggled. She had a few grazes and a twisted ankle and lay there surrounded by her friends, suitably sympathetic to her misfortune. I sat alongside her, gave her a hug and asked if she was okay. That was when the penny dropped that I was serious about her. Apparently her friends were not convinced of my affection, but after I left that afternoon they were all in agreement that I was for real. It was big news around school for a week or so.

We started dating after that, and I settled down a bit more at school. She was always on my case, asking if I was going to graduate or not. I would tell her, 'Of course I am', and she'd coolly shake her head and say she wondered how that was possible because she never saw me doing any work. I thought it was time to concentrate a bit more, and was determined to prove that, while I might have been a Pond Dog, I wasn't into a lot of the things some of my mates from the neighbourhood were into at the time. It was as if I had to work doubly hard to shake off the stigma attached to coming from the wrong side of town. She accepted me for who I was – eventually!

Back to football. There were other influences on my game around this time and most of them were from faraway shores. My friends and I were avid watchers of a TV football show called *Big League Soccer*, featuring matches from around the world, but from England in particular. My team was Liverpool, purely because of John Barnes who had become my idol. I watched him tear defences apart, glide past players and score spectacular goals, thinking all the while, 'That could be me – that little black kid playing for Liverpool could be me'. He had come from Jamaica and I wanted to emulate what he had achieved; he represented everything I wanted to be. Liverpool was my team, but being Bermudian and therefore fickle I also liked a couple of London clubs: West Ham and Tottenham. Both teams played the kind of football I loved and had players like Trevor Brooking, who was a stylish midfielder and had a certain grace about his play, and Garth Crooks, another black kid in whose footsteps I wanted to follow. I would watch as much *Big League Soccer* as I could, but it was those three players I particularly looked out for each week.

I also loved watching Brazilian and Argentinian football on the highlight shows at the Bascome house. We all loved the silky skills, technical ability and samba beat of South American football, and when Argentina played England in the 1986 World Cup I have to admit that we all ran into the streets when Maradona scored his second goal because it was just so beautiful to watch. He could run at people, leave them for dead, dribble, create and score – he was the ultimate entertainer, and for me the best footballer ever.

I was enjoying life, hanging out with my friends and playing as much football as daylight would allow. At school I graduated from Whitney Institute and was offered numerous full scholarships for various colleges, including one from Columbia High School in New Jersey, USA. A teacher there had a brother who taught soccer at Wake Forest University in North Carolina, and the idea was that I should attend Columbia High, get my SATs (grades needed to get into university) up to scratch and then attend college at Wake Forest. I graduated from Whitney with honours – yet my grades were average, at best, so I still can't work out where the honours bit comes from! The upshot was that to gain my scholarship I needed to bury my head in some books in New Jersey for a year and attend university in the States. So I left Bermuda to further my education and things went fine until I came across a stumbling block a couple of months into my internship: having played for my high school team in Bermuda, I was ineligible to play for Columbia High's soccer team, and that effectively meant a year with no competitive football. I was 17 and this was a time when, back home, I did little else but play so I had to ask myself some serious questions about whether I could stay the course. I knew that so long as I was able to play, my studies would go well and I would achieve my grades, but without regular games I was going to struggle.

At last the Thanksgiving break arrived and I returned home, already thinking that I would probably not be returning. It was November and it was a relief to get back to Bermuda, see my family and friends, and get a few games under my belt again. Playing football was all I knew and it was as if the break from involvement had polarised my thinking about where my future really lay. A life without football was a dull outlook, and not one I was about to embrace wholeheartedly.

Call it fate, coincidence or what you will, but on my return Manchester United just happened to be in Bermuda, because of a week-long break in their league programme. I was invited to play in a select XI against a Bermuda Under-21 side in a match prior to one of United's friendly clashes with the national team – it was known as a 'double-header' and was basically a support act to the big game. I played well enough, and seemingly had done enough to impress the United scouts, although I knew little about it at the time.

Whatever the reasons for their interest in me, this was what I had dreamed of, and I wasn't about to pass up such a chance. I travelled to Manchester for my trial period, then returned home and heard nothing for perhaps six months. I was certain that my chance had passed and was trying to put it out of my mind as best I could. Then, while I was in Haiti with the national team for a World Cup qualifier, I was handed a bombshell that would change my life for ever.

We were having a meeting in one of the swanky Haitian hotel rooms and I was chilling at the back, tilting my chair back, my legs up on a table, when the Bermuda coach at the time, Gary Darrell, said, 'I've got some good news – Shaun Goater's been offered a two-year contract with Manchester United'. I took my legs down and leaned forward. 'Say what?' He smiled and said, 'Congratulations, Shaun, United have offered you a two-year deal'. I didn't hear another word he said after that, because my mind was already in England, filled with being on the same pitch as players such as John Barnes, and I was so happy I could have jumped out of the window and into the pool below – and we were at least seven floors up! I was so excited that my dreams seemed to be coming true. I was going to play in England for Manchester United, and next time the guys back home watched *Big League Soccer* they would be watching me wheel away towards the

Stretford End after scoring my first goal for the club. I told Anita and after we had talked about it for hours she said I had to go and follow my dreams, and that she completely understood – which was typical of her. This wasn't the end for us, but being so far apart was bound to put a strain on our relationship. She later told me that leaving for England was the last thing she wanted me to do. She knew what football meant to me, because she'd seen me cry over the game after a poor performance for North Village ('What's up with you? It's only a game!'), and so she was with me all the way.

CHAPTER THREE

Cold Trafford

I travelled to England for my two-week trial with Manchester United with a man called Nick Jones, who was something of a national sports guru back home. He was involved in everything Bermudian and helped train a multitude of sportsmen and women for various competitions. I suppose he was something of a short-term chaperon for me and I will never forget his advice at an early United training session, when I had just two weeks to impress the coaches and secure a contract.

I limped to the sidelines with a knee injury and told Nick there was no way I could make the game the next day. He said, 'Well you'd better make yourself okay because you won't ever get a chance like this again'. As it turned out the knee was fine and I played in the game, scored a goal, and left hoping I'd done enough.

I returned home for about twelve months, resumed my career with North Village and worked as an apprentice surveyor for a short time while I waited for a work permit. It seemed like an eternity before I actually left Bermuda for Manchester. In July 1988 I arrived at Old Trafford to finally sign my contract with United. There were still a few formalities to be ironed out, and for a time I was getting about £40 a week to cover any expenses incurred. It wasn't long before I realised that I was on less money than the schoolkids who packed groceries back home. A youngster could earn around $30 a day packing bags in the food stores and when my real wage with United kicked in, at £130 a week I was still on virtually the same as any 10-year-old Bermudian grocery packer! So much for the imagined high life! I knew that if I was to make a career for myself in England I was going to have to start out on the bottom rung of the financial ladder, but this was ridiculous. Of course it wasn't really about the money, but I still needed to live, so I decided to go and see Alex Ferguson – who was still fairly new in the job himself.

'Gaffer,' I said to him, 'my mother and I have just bought a house in Bermuda and I've been helping her pay the mortgage and the money I get here is less than I earned back home.' He listened to me and said, 'Well, the best I can offer you, son, is £165'. I felt as if I had won the World Cup! I told him, 'I can work with that', and I did. In hindsight I think Fergie was just keeping me sweet until I moved on, because I don't believe for one minute that he or anyone else at the club really believed I had a long-term future there.

I got homesick fairly quickly and I used to call home regularly and speak with my family, but I was missing Anita a lot and phone calls didn't quite fill the void. We began sending tapes to each other, and with those we could listen to each other for up to an hour and catch up with everything that was happening at home and in Manchester. We would write long letters, too, and the old saying that absence makes the heart grow fonder is true, up to a point – but we knew before I left that what we had was solid.

I joined up with United's youth team and there were a lot of good players knocking around, but I never felt out of my depth, though I also reckoned I wasn't any better than the players they already had at the club. The lads in my age group were all British, which worried me. Why go to the trouble of fighting so hard for a work permit for a young player who was essentially the same as, perhaps, a 17-year-old based in Watford or Leeds? The only problem they would have was the time it would take their parents to drive them home – there was certainly no red tape to wade through. But by this stage, I had serious doubts as to whether they had plans to play me in the first team.

If I had been training with the first team, included in match-day squads and travelling with them, I would have thought differently about the whole situation; but I wasn't, except for rare occasions when I was given a taste by the gaffer. On one of these outings (countable on one hand) I travelled with the squad to Nottingham Forest. I distinctly recall being in a lounge area with the likes of Bryan Robson, Viv Anderson and Mark Hughes, and highlights of Liverpool on the TV with John Barnes in action – and at his very best. I watched, transfixed, as my hero left two for dead and slotted the ball into the net – and one of the lads got up and switched it off, mumbling that he 'didn't want to watch that rubbish'. I thought, 'Hey! What are you doing? That's John Barnes you're switching off. I could learn something – you could all learn something!' and despite its being a relatively big day for a young kid, I can't recall anything other than someone switching off John Barnes. I'm not sure whether that says more about me or about United! The whole day is a complete blur.

My first home in England was in digs in Salford, about 200 yards from The Cliff training ground. One particular day I was walking to a nearby shop for a packet of wine gums to chew on while watching TV and with me were fellow youth team players Lee Sharpe and Giuliano Maiorano. As we casually strolled along, a car pulled up across the road with two guys in it. One of them jumped out, went to the boot and said 'Hey, guys! I've got something for you'. Giuliano said 'Watch your backs' to Lee and me just as the man brought out a crowbar from the car. He looked at us, shouted 'I f***ing hate Man United!' and started chasing us down the street. I took one look at him and set off – there was no way he was going to catch me! Our Adidas tracksuits and proximity to The Cliff must have given away our identity as United youth players. He started yelling that he was a City fan, and even as I was running away I was thinking, 'What the hell's the matter with this guy?' I was aware of the rivalry between United and City, but not of its intensity, although years later I would happily immerse myself in it.

Lee Sharpe was my room-mate in digs and he was a great guy to be around. At Christmas I would be left alone in digs with my landlady Brenda Gosling and I would make a lot of calls back home. But Lee would often take me back to his parents' home in Birmingham at times when he knew I was alone, and I really got along well with both Lee and his family. I was playing for the A-team and the youth team at the time, and I remember one occasion when Mark Robins told me not to pass to a lad who was with us on trial. 'Don't pass to him,' he said, 'he's after taking our position'; but I was a little green and dismissed what he had said. Later, I went away and digested his comments and put it down to his experiences in this country. He knew how the system worked and I decided from then on to take more notice of what people were telling me and why.

I always used to play with a smile on my face and if I missed an easy chance I would grin and say to myself, 'God, Shaun, how did you miss that?' I did that until one game when Alex Ferguson said, 'If you smile again when you miss an opportunity you'll be on the first f***ing plane back to Bermuda'. I couldn't understand what the problem was and, looking back, Dwight Yorke arrived at about the same time as I did and he never lost his smile during his time at United – it was the laid-back culture we'd grown up in. I didn't find it funny that I had missed, or treat it as a joke; it was just a chuckle at myself.

For me, Fergie's warning was the beginning of becoming more businesslike on the pitch. He was warning me that this was my chance and not to blow it, and even if we did smile when we missed an opportunity in Bermuda, this was England and it was a completely different ball game. I never forgot Ferguson's words of wisdom, or, to put it more bluntly, threats.

There were many established stars at United while I was there – players like Mark Hughes, Brian McClair and Norman Whiteside, who was brilliant. There was one occasion when a mixture of the reserve and youth teams travelled to the Isle of Man and Norman came along too because he was recovering from injury. He decided to pay for a night out for all the lads and he knew I didn't drink, so when we arrived at a nightclub he said, 'Shaun, here's my wallet'. I asked him if he was sure and he replied, 'Yeah, yeah, absolutely', and instructed me that all the drinks were on him. Then he paid for the lads to have an Indian meal and nothing was a problem – rounds of drinks, anything. He knew most of us couldn't afford to be too lavish, whereas he could, and his generosity proved what a genuine guy he was. Despite a heavy night on the town Norman would be first up while I was exhausted! He also invited me to his house, knowing that I was on my own and far away from home, which I appreciated.

I went along to Norman's with Lee Sharpe and you couldn't help but be impressed by the house. It was filled with gadgets, intercoms in all the rooms, and a snooker room. I looked around and thought, 'Yeah, this is what I want! This is what I came here for!' I was really grateful for the way he treated me. He was a top player, too. One morning at training for the reserves, we were about to begin an eleven-a-side game when he came up to me and said, 'I'm not going to lose the ball in this match' – and he didn't. In Norman, I could see exactly how far I would have to go to get anywhere near the top, because he was simply in a different league.

Some of the younger players were coming through, and obviously Fergie felt he could dispense with certain members of his squad. Mark Bosnich, Mark Robins, Lee Martin and Lee Sharpe were all breaking into the senior squad. Yet there wasn't the merest hint there was any future for me. I had already figured that if I was going to make it in England I would have to move on. I wanted to make the most of my time at Old Trafford, though, and watch some great strikers in action, ask advice and be taught by some great coaches. I had to make the most of the opportunity I had and take from it what I could.

I needed to see how they made their runs and when, learn my role and discover what was expected of me in the English game. As for Fergie, well, he was and still is a top manager. He would come and watch all levels and age groups playing and there would be times when you had finished a reserve match and he would appear in the dressing room, hammer you if things weren't going well and then leave. In fact, I often wondered just how much he noticed me around the club, but the truth is, I think he notices everyone and everything. Not much gets past him, that's for sure.

I used to fool around in the canteen, entertaining the other lads and doing a spot of shadow boxing, taking a few imaginary hits for a laugh. Years later I saw Fergie and he asked if I still did my stuff around the canteen, and I was taken aback. I suppose it was his business to notice everything, and even if it wasn't he made sure it was. Having said that, I'm not sure he recalled anything I'd done on the pitch!

Towards the end of my time at Old Trafford Jesper Olsen and Paul Ince were signed, but it was when Mark Hughes rejoined from Barcelona that I really noticed what an effect a major star could have at a club. He would walk into the canteen and there would almost be silence and I thought, 'Yeah, that's the daddy all right'. He was the main man, even if nobody actually said as much. Sometimes I would say to Mark, 'When are you going to get me some tracksuits, man?' I still had my street personality and wasn't afraid of reputations. 'Come on, man, you're hooked up with Adidas, sort me out', and he would say, 'Yeah, Shaun, I'll get you something. I'm on it'. He never got me one, though! It's a shame, because all I had ever worn was tracksuits and it would have been nice to increase my wardrobe with a quality Adidas tracky that I could have saved for special occasions.

I used to get along with most people at the club, but I do recall Steve Bruce coming into the boot room on one occasion and saying, 'Do you clean my boots? My boots aren't clean and you should make sure they're done properly'. I looked around and there was nobody else about, so I just said, 'You've got me mixed up with somebody else because I don't clean your boots'. If he was looking to make me feel small I wasn't having it, even though I know some of the other young lads would have just taken them away and cleaned them, regardless. That was the only sour note of my time at United. I have seen Steve several times since and he has never been less than brilliant – although I doubt he would remember our boot room 'chat'.

City beat United 5–1 at Maine Road in September 1989. The United fans were calling for Fergie's head and, in truth, he was probably close to the sack during that season. I was part of a reserve team that was doing really well at that point and I thought that it was either now or never for me. I waited for the call, but it never came. Ferguson went with Deniol Graham and Mark Robins for a couple of games and that told me all I needed to know. I had watched my mate Lee Sharpe start to make his way in the first team and seen the gradual change in him and in his mentality, from being just another number to an aura that suggested 'I'm not just another number – I'm part of the plans'. His appearance changed, he bought a sports car and he was shopping in smart shops. We were still in digs together, but we were now a million miles apart career-wise. It was weird because I always thought Giuliano Maiorano was a better player than Lee, but Maiorano had a mouth on him and it soon became clear he had no future under Ferguson, who didn't tolerate anybody talking back to him. Lee was given a chance to develop at the top level, and although it took time he eventually became a regular first teamer. If I had been given my chance, would I have succeeded? Who can say? I think, given a decent run, I would have, but I needed somebody to believe in me and stick by me, and that never happened.

So with no sniff of first-team football and no encouragement from the manager or coaching staff, I knew it was time to quit Manchester United. I think I had gone as far as I could, and although I had learned a lot in my short time there, I needed to move on to continue my education. Maybe I just wasn't ready to be thrown in at the deep end. One thing I was sure of, however: there was no way I was going to leave England without having a real crack at it somewhere. I wasn't prepared to hop on a plane to Bermuda having failed to get to the top level, whichever route I was going to have to take. Sure, I was missing home, and at Christmas it was especially tough, but I learned to get past that by looking to the future – and I was about to discover that it lay less than 40 miles away across the Pennines, in the small Yorkshire town of Rotherham. It was at Millmoor that I would really begin my apprenticeship in English football, and the contrast between Rotherham United and Manchester United could not have been greater.

CHAPTER FOUR

The Sun Ain't Gonna Shine Anymore

Alex Ferguson called me into his office to tell me there was a club interested in me. When you are playing at a top-level club, your mind only thinks about other teams in your division. Wrong.

Ferguson told me it was Rotherham United who had come in with an offer and I thought, 'Oh, Rotherham. Great – who are they?' I didn't know who they were, where they were or what division they played in. I just didn't follow football except United and the top league sides. I paid no attention to the second, third or fourth divisions because I had no need to. My first question was, where were they in England, and Fergie told me they were a hard-working outfit willing to give me first-team football. He added that I could learn the game with them because I wasn't going to get a chance at United. I had to give him credit – he didn't mince his words or try to dress things up, he just told me the bare facts. It was not a time when agents dominated football, so I had to make the decision on my own. I went back to my digs and thought about it and eventually decided it would be for the best if I did join Rotherham. As Fergie had said, I needed to serve my apprenticeship and adjust to the English game, and I thought 'Why not?' I checked out their geographical location and their league status and thought 'Oh, God, they're in the Third Division!' I was dropping a couple of levels. Undeterred, I reckoned if I could go to Rotherham for a couple of years, learn a bit about the game and then move back up, it would not be so bad. In my head it seemed quite simple, but it wasn't to be the case at all, and my apprenticeship very nearly became a prison term.

My mum, sister Juanita and Anita had flown to England to come with me to sign for Rotherham and we were all at Piccadilly station in Manchester waiting for our train. There was a little bit of sunshine on the bench where we sat, and we were all edging out of the shade and into the shaft of sunlight because we found it so bitterly cold. We must have looked comical sitting there, bunched up, blowing our hands, trying to keep warm. Little was I to know that the freezing temperatures would seem almost year-round in Rotherham.

John Breckin was the reserve manager and he picked us up from the station and took me to a digs in the town. I had wondered how this move had come about, and could only think that Ferguson must have called Billy McEwan at Rotherham to offer my services and that there was some kind of Scottish connection between them. I couldn't see that Rotherham had scouted me because there wouldn't have been much chance to see me in action, and I doubted I had done anything special since I'd been in England. I left a club that gave you the ball regardless of whether you were being closely marked for a team that wouldn't pass to you if you had anyone within 5 yards. 'Give me the ball!'

'No! We'll knock it in behind you' – and so it went on. I thought they were kidding me, and it was quite a shock to the system after being in such a cultured environment at Old Trafford.

The training was very basic and very hard – trust me – but I was enthusiastic and although the sun wasn't shining I was playing football, and that was all I was concerned about for the first twelve months. The second season was much harder and the running sessions each Monday were completely joyless, bordering on torturous, and more often than not would end with me being physically sick. This was old school and then some, and I used to detest it. I was beginning to think that this wasn't all it was cracked up to be. At United, we did running, but only with such intensity in pre-season, and this was every week, whether we won 6–0 or lost 6–0. The theory at Rotherham was that we weren't good enough to keep the ball, so we had to be fit enough to win it back. I had serious thoughts of packing it in and returning home. In Bermuda I wouldn't have found it hard to earn more money, and here in Rotherham the sun never seemed to shine and it was perpetually cold.

When the frost and ice came I secretly rejoiced because I thought training would be cancelled (if you got just a few spots of rain in Bermuda the session was cancelled), but I discovered that training was never cancelled at Rotherham. Ever.

We played British bulldog one morning where the lads come at you en masse and, unless you can dodge them quickly enough, they smash you to the floor. It was designed to toughen you up, but I just stood over in the corner and the lads shouted, 'Shaun's out, he's out of bounds'. I was devastated about that – it took me seconds to get over it! Another time they had shirts versus skins and the temperature was minus one. Not being a fan of hypothermia, I wouldn't take my top off, and they told me I was soft – but I wasn't bothered, I wanted to stay soft because I wasn't adjusting to the weather. I once rolled a snowball and the pain shot up my arm. Even after the session had finished and the lads were showered and gone, I still sat waiting for my hands to thaw out and the pins and needles to stop.

So many bad things seemed to be happening that a voice inside my head said 'Quit, quit, quit, quit', but that was the last thing I really wanted to do. I didn't want to go back home having failed. If I returned to Bermuda it would be because Rotherham thought I wasn't good enough.

There were many mornings when I would open the curtains and hail would be striking the window and it would be dark outside. If it was a Monday running session in a few hours, all I wanted to do was go back to bed and curl up. Actually playing for the club wasn't any easier. This was a working-class area and the people who came to watch had worked hard to earn their money. If they were spending it to watch us play football, they expected nothing less than 100 per cent effort, or they would let you know in no uncertain terms – and Rotherham fans could moan with a passion. I used to think, 'Why are you not happy?' but that was who they were and what they were about. It wasn't personal, they were just hardy souls.

The supporters had plenty to moan about at the end of season 1991/92, as the club were relegated to the Fourth Division, although I was pleased with my return of nine goals in twenty-four league games; and though we came straight back up, I hadn't done fantastically well with only seven goals in twenty-three league matches. I had been at the club about four years before I finally got it into my head that I had to forget the sun, forget the adverse weather and forget Bermuda. This was what life in England's Third Division was like, and once I changed my thinking and let all that go I began producing and scoring more frequently.

Yet despite this, I know they tried to get rid of me to nearby Chesterfield in late 1993. It was before I had changed my mindset and realised I had to knuckle down and get on with it, but Chesterfield were interested and I went along to meet their manager, John Duncan. Phil Henson, who had taken over from Billy McEwan in 1991, told me I wasn't part of his plans, so I thought that if I was moving somewhere so close to Rotherham I would be paid the appropriate rate. When they asked me what I was looking for I said somewhere in the region of £700 – which was about £300 more than I was currently on. I felt I had nothing to lose because I didn't want to sign for them anyway. Duncan said, 'We can't pay you that, son', so I told them that in that case they didn't really want me. Chesterfield's selling point was that I would grow and develop with them and eventually move on, but I wasn't buying it – to me, it was just another Rotherham. I didn't realise it at the time, but I was serving my dues and giving myself a grounding that would prove invaluable in later years.

Henson must have got wind of another club's interest, because he began playing me more often before Notts County came in for me. They took me on loan and were in Division Two, a league higher and doing well, too. They had some decent players, such as Andy Legg and Tony Agana, and I made my debut in a 2–1 defeat at Charlton, managing to set up the Notts goal. Their next game was in the Anglo-Italian Cup against Italian side Brescia and I was suitably impressed: European football in only my second game with them! I had a pre-match meal of pasta, which was probably the first time I had eaten the right food before a match, and I could see that Notts County were a well-run outfit. Things seemed to be looking up.

I went back to the hotel to rest up before the match, and received a phone call from the club secretary saying that he had looked into everything and I wasn't eligible to play in the game. I said, 'Sorry, what's that?' He told me I could not continue my loan with the club because I needed a separate work permit – my current permit only allowed me to play for Rotherham. I couldn't believe it. I was gutted. Hours before I played my first match in Europe, and it was taken away from me. Although I didn't know it at the time, that was the nearest I ever got to playing football in European competition. I still travelled with the team for the experience.

I returned to Rotherham and things finally began to take off for me. Whether the interest from other clubs had given them a change of heart or whether they had seen a change in me I'm not sure, but I was put straight back into the first team and it remained pretty much that way for the rest of my career at Millmoor. Playing for Notts County had given me belief and the confidence I needed, because they were flying in a division higher and still wanted me to play for them. If they were so keen I knew I could hack it a level below – and flourish. And at last that's exactly what I did.

I started scoring goals for Rotherham and finally began to feel more at home in England. Anita had moved over to be with me by this time and we got our first home – a one-up, one-down at 98 Fleming Way, Wickersley. It was a decent area – unless you went around the corner, where the neighbourhood took a definite downturn and, if you were really unlucky, you might meet Rotherham's own version of a Pond Dog. We had Economy heaters around the house that didn't come on at night and would wake in the morning almost seeing frost on our breath as we exhaled. More often than not we hid back under the covers. Anita saw ice on the inside of the bedroom window one day and asked what it was because she'd never seen it before – at least not *inside* a house. I told her that was our homemade barometer and it was reading 'bloody freezing'. Anita later told me that it was moments like that that made her realise how much she loved me, because any sane person would have jumped on the first plane home to Bermuda.

We still looked forward to our return to Bermuda for the summer, and it was on one such visit that I met someone who would help shape my future and also become a close friend and confidant. David Bascome and I were entrepreneurs, always coming up with one scheme or another, and we approached the famous Front Street department store Trimminghams to do some work. We suggested that we model various items of sportswear in a fashion show they were holding on the premises and they thought it was a good idea with our background in professional sport. They paid us $750 to do a bit on the catwalk, which was good money at the time.

A man at the event came over and introduced himself to us as a fan of English football, explaining that he was a Coventry City supporter and had seen me play several times for Rotherham. His name was Mark Georgevic, and he had lived and worked in Bermuda with his family for several years. He seemed a good guy who knew his stuff. I would bump into him every now and then around Hamilton, and on one occasion he suggested I should look into acquiring tapes of Rotherham's games and getting them replayed on Bermudian TV. I thought that was a great idea because it would give people back home a chance to see how my career was progressing in England. There was a great deal of interest in how I was doing but little TV coverage, and this would be the perfect solution, perhaps even inspiring Bermudian youngsters by showing them what was possible with the right work ethic. Mark looked into it for me, secured the sponsorship to make it happen, and before long the tapes started arriving. Once the tapes had been converted to Bermudian format we were all set and ready to air.

Mark was involved with every aspect of the scheme and even did the commentary as if it were a live match, me adding my own comments in the third person. It was funny, because I sometimes had to pass an opinion on something I had done – or not done – and it would be along the lines of 'The ball comes into Shaun – what a wasted opportunity that was! He'll really be upset with himself there!'

We did that for close on a year and got some great feedback from the show. It certainly helped to raise my profile back home, and Mark did everything in his spare time for no payment. We became good friends and Mark was much more than a would-be John Motson. In his day job he was a lawyer – and a damned good one at that. He suggested that I start a company and gave me some very sound advice about the future. Everything I had done up to that point was without representation. Initially I thought, 'Well, what does he want?' He said he didn't want anything at all – we just got on well and I valued his opinion.

He returned later to England and it was around then that he became my agent and adviser. He knew his stuff and was first class with contracts and legalities, so I thought, 'Why not?' I needed somebody I could trust, he had become a good friend and it would prove to be one of the best decisions I made in my career. I never signed a thing with Mark, it was a contract based on each other's word, and as my career began to take off he left the door open for me to get other representation if I wanted it – but I never did. I could not imagine finding anyone better to represent me.

Back at Rotherham, where the fans had christened me 'Lenny', I was scoring freely and my confidence was high. From 1994/95 onwards I was the club's leading scorer, twice managing to top the 20-goal mark, and I got on well with Phil Henson. In 1995/96 the board took the unusual step of appointing a joint management team of John McGovern and Archie Gemmill. Not entirely coincidentally this turned out to be my last season in South Yorkshire.

At least my final season also provided the proudest moment of my career so far. Undoubtedly the highlight of my time with the Millers was reaching the 1996 Auto Windscreens final against Shrewsbury Town. As a kid I had dreamed of playing at Wembley Stadium, having watched so many FA Cup finals. I had imagined what it must be like walking out of the tunnel with the rest of the team and being greeted by a wall of noise, seeing all the flags waving. It was a milestone in my career and a great day for Bermuda because I was the first from my country to play there. The day seemed to whizz by all too quickly. I tried to soak it all in. The 8 foot-deep bath, the cavernous dressing rooms, our own barman serving soft drinks. This was Rotherham's first Wembley final and there was a crowd of almost 40,000. As I looked around I had a thought: 'Virtually all of Bermuda is in this stadium . . . there's nobody at home.'

My first impression of the Wembley pitch was that it was not as good as it looked on TV and was not the bowling green I had expected. I suppose it wasn't bad, though! I tried to spot Anita, as well as Kyle Lightbourne and his wife Rosemarie, in the crowd, but I can recall little in the way of actual match action, probably because of nerves, although I did help lay on the winning goal for Nigel Jemson. We won 2–1. It was a fantastic feeling, walking up those famous steps to get our winners' medals.

One of my after-match quotes proved I had got lost in the moment as I told a reporter, 'You'd better watch out, there's a new United in town – Rotherham United!' The reaction came, 'Steady on, son', then, 'Are you sure he doesn't drink?'

But something happened on the coach home that I couldn't – or wouldn't – ever forget. It took me totally by surprise and made my mind up that wherever I ended up the following season, it wouldn't be Rotherham United.

We were in traffic and a car drew alongside us with some girls inside. All the lads came across, ogling them and banging on the window. There were various shouts from the lads – typical stuff – and I was behind a few of the guys trying to look at what they were looking at. Suddenly, Archie Gemmill marched up from the rear of the coach and heard one of the lads say something along the lines of, 'Get your tits out!' to the girls. Gemmill looked at me and bawled me out in a personally insulting way, saying that the girl in the car was his daughter. The only thing was, I hadn't shouted anything. All the lads were shocked, looking at each other with stunned expressions. It was a strange situation because it was the manager who had said this and he had singled me out, despite my being nowhere near the front. Surely he knew it hadn't been me?

I was taken aback at such a blatant display of what was little less than racism, and was at a loss what do next because this was my gaffer. We had just won the Auto Windscreens Trophy and had been celebrating our success, the biggest day in the club's history – and this killed the moment completely. I said, 'Gaffer, that wasn't me that shouted that, and if the lads had known it was your daughter they wouldn't have shouted anything'. It was left at that for the time being. The lads told me not to worry about it and to forget it ever happened, but half an hour or so later I was started to boil over and I thought, 'Nah, I'm not having that'.

I couldn't let what he had said just ride, and the following morning I went into his office and said, 'I don't appreciate what you said and I don't appreciate you coming and singling me out in front of the lads and saying what you said. Now I want you to apologise to me in front of the lads'. It was a pivotal moment in my life, a rite of passage if you like, because this was something I had to sort out myself. It was a situation I had not expected to find myself in – but, to his credit, he did exactly what I'd asked.

He apologised, saying he had acted in the heat of the moment and had genuinely thought it was me. I accepted the apology but reiterated that I wanted it said in front of the other players.

It was just before training and nobody knew I had been to see Gemmill in his office. A few minutes later he came into the changing rooms and said, 'Gather round, lads, there's something I want to say. I'd just like to say to Shaun in front of you all that I apologise for what I said yesterday. It was wrong of me and I jumped on him and accused him, and for that I apologise and I hope you can accept it. It wasn't meant and was a reaction to the moment.'

I nodded and said I accepted what he was saying, but it was still a bitter pill to swallow because I'd been at the club for six years and the last three had been good. I was a senior member of the team and I had the respect of my teammates but, heat of the moment or not, Gemmill had still felt he could speak to me in the way he had.

John McGovern was a neighbour of mine, and when he moved in he invited me round for tea and I met his family. He was absolutely brilliant. At the end of the season the club informed me they were not offering improved terms for season 1996/97, and with the Gemmill tirade still fresh in my mind I decided I would never play for Rotherham United again.

I had learned a lot about the game with them and met some great people. The fans were hard, but fair, and although they always wanted more from you I always knew where I stood with them, and I suppose they kept me on my toes. I had also learned some valuable lessons about life and been given tips that helped improve my game tremendously. Bobby Williamson and Clive

Mendonca were a great help. Bobby was the first person to tell me about the near-post run, and his advice when we played together was invaluable because I got a lot more joy and many more goals through implementing it in my game.

Mark Dempsey, Imre Varadi and Nigel Jemson – good players who'd seen better days elsewhere, but still had much to offer. One lad I will never forget from my days there was Ally Pickering. Ally was a real character. He arrived after me and in one of his first games he said, 'It's like a f***ing morgue out there – what's wrong with us?' He wasn't being cocky, just confident. He was a Manchester lad and this was only his second game for us, but I could see he had been given a chance at Rotherham and was not going to let it pass him by. His comments that day were right, too. Although we knew we were too quiet, nobody had the guts to say it.

I liked him straight away. He was a Manchester City fanatic – he would arrive for training in City shirt and shorts and say they were the best team in the world and sing 'City till I Die'. He was just mad on that club. I would say, 'Who the hell are City? No one's heard of them!' and Ally would reply that you didn't know football if you didn't know anything about City. We carried this on for months, until he moved on to Coventry. Who were Manchester City indeed? If only I had known what the future had in store for me . . . For now, I had to sort out where I would be playing next season.

CHAPTER FIVE

Bristol Fashion

I had come to the end of my contract at Rotherham and, having scored almost fifty goals in two years, I felt my stock was rising and now was as good a time as any to move on. The Bosman ruling was just coming into effect, which was good for me as it released the shackles I had been in for some time now. Before that, you could be out of contract but the club could still hold your registration. Manchester United was due a percentage of any sell-on fee, which had been killing my chances of leaving the club.

I had been at Millmoor for six years and given the club good value for money, but it had become Groundhog Day and not much had changed since my arrival; I couldn't see any way things would improve. Things had come to a head, time was moving on, and I desperately needed a new challenge to test myself at the next level.

I left for Bermuda, unsure of the future and intending to return only if nothing better came along. It was always good to get home after months of drizzle and cold. Within a few weeks I was totally relaxed, enjoying the sunshine, and also had something to take my mind off football for a little while. A year earlier I had finally got round to asking Anita to be my wife, and on 17 May 1996 we were married at St John's Church in Bailey's Bay. We had been to a wedding there some time back and enjoyed the day, and decided that was the place we wanted to wed. David Bascome was my best man. Only a few close friends and family members were invited – it was about the occasion of marriage and nothing more.

It was also out of Hamilton, where everyone knew me from back of town to the Pond, and it was a case of locating the reception in a place where people I knew wouldn't just turn up on spec for a plate of food and a dance. We chose St Georges, a place overlooking the water, ten minutes away from the church. Much as I enjoyed the day, I was glad when it was all over and we could rest up. It had been enjoyable, but stressful and tiring too. The next day we hopped on a plane to Florida and caught the East Coast Caribbean cruise, which was lovely. We ended our honeymoon with a five-day stay in New York, which we had always wanted to visit – but had never got around to.

Rotherham, and the problems I was having there, seemed a million miles away as we visited the Statue of Liberty, shopped in Manhattan, and did all the tourist stuff. Returning to the island, I chilled out, caught up with family and friends – and there was always the soccer camp to organise. But the pace of life was so leisurely I could immerse myself in what I call Bermuda Time, when the clock ticks that little bit more slowly. In fact, I enjoyed myself too much and put on about 13 pounds in weight, but I knew it wouldn't be the Monday morning runs in Rotherham where I would be losing it.

I had passed on my affairs to Mark Georgevic by the time pre-season approached and he had begun to act on my behalf. He called me a few weeks into the break to tell me Spanish side Osasuna were showing an interest in signing me and had invited me over to take a look around. I considered it because I felt the Spanish style would suit my game – and the money was great. They were willing to pay me £3,000 a week – almost five times what I'd been on at Millmoor. But I had other concerns to think of. Anita had been in England for four years and had adjusted to the English way of life and it was important that she was happy, too. A move to Spain would have meant settling into a new country all over again and learning the language, and I just wasn't prepared to do that, so despite the tempting pay packet I turned down the offer.

I was amazed when Samsung FC, a South Korean club, offered me the chance to play for them in May 1996. I seriously thought about going and trying a completely different way of life for a while – I even bought books on the place! They were keen to bring players over from European clubs as the Korean Republic and Japan were due to host the World Cup in 2002, and though the terms were decent, for one reason or another it never came off, but I do wonder which way my career would have gone if I had moved there.

I then learned that Bristol City were interested, and this was like sweet music to my ears. From the moment I found out I pretty much decided that I was going there, whatever the financial terms. Even if they had offered less money than Rotherham I would still have signed for them. I had served a lengthy apprenticeship and proved I could hack it in England. Now a much bigger club was willing to take a chance on me and it was the shot in the arm my career desperately needed.

On our return to England I took Anita to Bristol to have a look round. As soon as we arrived and saw the seagulls and the water, we knew this was the right thing to do. It was a warm, sunny day and Bristol had a pleasant town centre and I thought, 'This is the closest thing to Bermuda I've seen'. I was very happy with everything and by the time I went to meet the club's representatives, mentally I was already a Bristol City player. As we walked around town nobody recognised me or said anything, but I made myself a little promise that by the time I left the club everyone in this city would know who I was. If that happened it would mean I had achieved my goal and been a success.

Bristol were trying to sell the club to me, saying that I should really give the chance of joining them a lot of thought and that I would really enjoy playing for them, and all the while I thought, 'This is a done deal!' Mark and chairman Scott Davidson invited Anita and me for a meal at a swanky restaurant in town. The food was a little too fancy for our liking – transparent noodles and such. We picked at the food and later headed to McDonalds because we were starving! The chairman told me about the club's plans and its fantastic fan base. They were capable of filling Ashton Gate and averaged around 14,000, which was treble the crowd I was used to playing in front of.

The financial aspects were ironed out, but if my wages at Rotherham had been £600, the rise at Bristol City wasn't anything dramatic – say another £150. But I was determined to sign for them, come what may. It had a lot to do with appreciation and a feeling of being wanted – the surroundings were nice too, but as a player you need to feel that you are special sometimes, and that's how Bristol City made me feel. I was to replace Andy Cole, who had left for Newcastle United in a mega-money deal about six months earlier, and he had had a great season and been a big crowd favourite. I knew that I was expected to find the net regularly, and if I continued the good form of the past couple of years there was no reason why I shouldn't do exactly that.

There was a definite feel-good factor about the whole thing – and the missus was happy! In fact, before long Anita was socialising with the other players' wives, something that had never happened before. We moved to Nailsea, a nice area near Bristol, and the club paid £175,000 to Rotherham for my services and a percentage of that went to Manchester United – although it probably wouldn't even have paid Eric Cantona's wages for a week. I signed the contract and met up with the rest of the squad for the first day of pre-season training. My summer schedule was fairly simple. I did nothing at all when I was in Bermuda except have a good time, relax and eat whatever I wanted – it's known as The Goat Plan! I remember meeting the lads, and the first few runs manager Joe Jordan took us on I ended up getting lost because I was so far behind. All that rich living back home had caught up on me!

I set myself little targets to build up my fitness slowly. During the runs I would check out who was generally the one in front of me and aim to be within a certain distance of him next time around. If he had beaten me by half a lap the first time, by the second run I would aim to be about 15 yards behind him at the finish and gradually build up my fitness. No doubt the staff must have thought, 'What have we signed here?' Assistant manager Gerry Sweeney took us out a lot and although he was a lot older than I he was twice as fit. By the end of pre-season I would be third or fourth last instead of lagging way behind, and so long as I achieved that I was happy because I knew I had reached a fair level of fitness. I wasn't good at long-distance running, but when it came to sprints I was always the best – that was my strength. Running to a tree 3 miles away and back just wasn't for me.

My game was based around anticipation and being quick off the mark, and a lot of my goals were scored by being first to a ball, which would give me the chance to maybe toe-poke the ball home ahead of the man who was marking me. Being sharp and alert helped me score a lot of goals.

They were a good bunch of lads at Bristol and they made me feel at home from day one. I can honestly say there was no one with whom I didn't feel I got along on the playing staff. One lad I quickly bonded with was Greg Goodridge, a pacy winger with an eye for a goal who joined us a couple of weeks into the season. Greg was from Barbados and we hit it off initially because we shared the same taste in music – a bit of reggae or R&B – and we were similar in a lot of ways. Greg would dress as we did on the streets back home and his three-quarter length jeans, ankle socks and trainers would invariably be the butt of the lads' jokes at training. 'You run out of material there, Greg?' Brian Tinnion was one of the lead mischief-makers; I bumped into him a couple of years ago, and guess what he was wearing? Three-quarter length pants! So Greg and I hit it off and we would have a laugh about our international tussles. I would say, 'Bring in that tape of me scoring against Barbados for the lads', but he would have none of it and gave me back as good as he got.

I also got along well with Junior Bent, who had done the rounds at a few clubs. He was a little, short guy, and a great lad too. If those guys became good mates off the pitch, on it there were two players alongside whom it was fantastic to play. Brian Tinnion and Darren Barnard were two of the best left-sided players I have ever played with, and even when I later signed for Manchester City I wondered why they had never played at a higher level. They were good for me and they understood my game to such a degree that I couldn't do anything but succeed at Ashton Gate. They supplied accurate crosses to me for fun, but I realised that I was good for Tinnion too, because I understood what he was aiming to do when he was on the ball. Barnard could take a fantastic free kick from anywhere around the box and he would cause problems. Although he later moved to Barnsley in a big-money deal he never reached the heights his talent deserved.

On the right wing was the flashy Goodridge, full of tricks, step-overs and dummies. Greg couldn't just beat his man and move on, he would have to do a step-over, make some space and then smash the ball across the box, and unless I was within a yard or two of those crosses I would struggle to get there. He was equally capable of cutting inside and hammering the ball into the roof of the net as well, and was especially renowned for his long throw-ins. Anita has always been a good observer of the game and I always listened to her advice. She saw Greg play and told me that she thought I should make more noise on the pitch – she didn't mean vocally, either. She saw how Greg would use his skill to make a defender look silly, and if he did go and smash the ball home Anita said that was Greg making some noise. She felt I needed to do something to draw attention to myself, and I knew what she meant, because you couldn't help but notice Greg when he played. If I was going to make my own noise it would have to be in the form of goals on a bigger platform.

My first game for Bristol City was a final against Bristol Rovers for the ninety-ninth Gloucestershire Senior Cup, and I scored a goal but pulled up a lot with cramp. I still needed to improve my sharpness, but was happy to find the net so early on, and I think that scoring against Rovers certainly helped my credit rating with the fans.

I had been really looking forward to working under Joe Jordan. He had been a top striker for Leeds, Manchester United, Juventus and Scotland, and was a man who could take my game up to the next level. I looked forward to the advice and tips he would give me and to having him coaching me on the training pitch; I could learn a lot from him. As it turned out I learned very little, which still disappoints me to this day. I later found out that it was Scott

Davidson, the chairman, who brought me to the club, but at the time I thought Jordan had gone for me because he rated me as a forward.

My game was never going to be like Jordan's, but he had been a striker. During training sessions he concentrated on defence and I would think, 'God, this is killing me!' He would work on defending from the front, and have me and my strike partner running across the back four and shadowing them, and all the while I would be thinking, 'When are you going to do something with the strikers?' I was desperate to work with him and to learn as much as I could, and I could never work out why it never really happened.

The season finally began for real, and I managed to score on my debut at Gillingham. We lost 3–2, but it was an encouraging start and I remember scoring my goal – a header from a right-wing cross in front of about 1,500 of our fans, and they were going absolutely mad. It was a great feeling to get off the mark so early in my career and gave me the confidence I needed to go on and do well. I scored again in my second game, a 3–3 draw at Torquay. I have always started the season well throughout my career, and I can only put it down to the weather. August is often nice and sunny and the pitches are hard, which was all I had ever known before I came to England. It was Bermudian conditions for me, and I don't think anyone should underestimate what an advantage something like that can be – if the player believes it, of course. In those conditions I could read situations better and predict how the ball would bounce, and while other players might have been sweating in the English sun, I just thought, 'This ain't hot! It's not even warm!'

I settled in very quickly and was wearing my favourite No. 10 jersey in honour of one Diego Armando Maradona – the greatest number ten that's ever lived. Pele also wore No. 10, as did John

Barnes, and I was happy to be in such exalted company. I liked that shirt, but was not so keen on the No. 9. In England it is reserved for the powerful forward who puts his weight around and dives on to the end of crosses to plant headers into the back of the net. You might as well have given me the No. 34 shirt in that case, because that was definitely not my game.

I continued my scoring run during a 5–0 home win over Luton, to make it three in four games, and the fans seemed to be happy enough with me, nicknaming me 'Billy'. We ticked along well and in September I returned to Rotherham for my first game against them. I found that game really tough, and that pattern continued in future meetings; I always struggled to score against them. There were only about 2,500 fans there and it was a mixed reception; I wondered what they were thinking of me now I had left. The boos I took to be a compliment because I thought that if they didn't care they wouldn't do anything at all, so I hoped that the jeers were because of missing me – but that's me, always looking on the positive side. At the end of the campaign Rotherham were relegated and the thought must have crossed the board's mind that if they had given me a decent pay offer my goals might have kept them up.

I added a couple more goals against Walsall – finally taking a win bonus off my old mate Kyle Lightbourne, who had always got the better of me up till then – before scoring a couple against Burnley, a team I thought of throughout my career as a Direct Debit, because I always seemed to deposit a couple of goals into their account. It's strange how you can score against certain teams but have difficulty against others. Burnley were easily the best and most fruitful for me, whereas Chesterfield were a side I couldn't find the net against until my last season in league football! So, with seven goals in twelve games I was doing okay, although I then went five without managing to score once! The Goat's cure for barren runs is a hat-trick, which was what I managed against

Notts County to move into double figures for the season and add another match ball to my collection – if only I had done that every time I struggled to find the net.

We signed Clayton Blackmore on loan for a few months and I wondered whether he remembered me from our days together at United, but he was always fine with me and did not stay that long before moving on again.

As for strike partners, I used to enjoy playing alongside Kevin Nugent because he would do all the aerial work and provide me with decent knock-downs. On occasion I would play with Paul Agostini, a decent striker who had a penchant for overhead kicks, none of which, as I recall, ever bore fruit. He would try the spectacular when sometimes a simple header would suffice; it was as if he was on a mission to score with a bicycle kick. I am more basic in my thinking, and if I try something that is not coming off I look at the numbers; if I am not scoring goals, I just drop it and stick to the tried and tested. He scored a few times, but moved on to Germany after a while. But between the two I preferred big Kevin, without a doubt.

I got on well with everyone, but I remember having a barney with Brian Tinnion in one game that went on throughout the match. We disagreed about who should have been closing down a full-back, and after a while I decided that, as a striker, I needed to conserve some energy. Tinnion said that if I didn't do what he considered to be my job he would 'knock my block off!' If he felt that way, I told him, he knew where I would be at half-time. We might have had our disagreements, but there was great respect on the field. I blamed Jordan for that type of fall-out because he was so obsessed with defending from the front. If he had given back a bit more to the strikers, maybe we could have got on with the job we were paid for – scoring goals – instead of bickering about defensive play.

I continued knocking in goals here and there, but on 1 February 1997 we travelled to Millwall, and my opinion of that club is that it should have been closed down a long time ago. I cannot understand how black players can play for Millwall and back then I just thought they were a joke. The abuse black players got – and still do, as far as I know – was a disgrace and the authorities should have brought them to task many years ago.

It was always a game I was happy to have behind me, and on this particular day we were told there would be a delay in leaving as there was trouble outside the ground. Because of the result, they had slipped further into trouble at the bottom of the table and the fans were smashing up cars, fighting with police, and we were stuck in the players' lounge, eager to get on our way. I felt threatened and was concerned for our fans' safety as we waited. The next thing we knew about a half dozen of their fans made it up to the lounge – big, heavy skinheads – and the first thing I thought was, 'They're coming for the black boys'. As it transpired, they made their way to their own players, but it was a really terrifying moment. Because they were so angry with their own team they left us alone. We turned our backs and waited for things to die down – or kick off.

I have played at Millwall when they have scored and the fans have run onto the pitch. It's a frightening experience. Setting out to intimidate, more often than not they succeed. We didn't know whether they were carrying knives when they ran on, and in an after-match interview I said that I had been scared for my own safety and that of my teammates. That was twisted in the press to 'Goater calls kids racist!' I didn't care whether they were kids or not, all I knew was that they were bigger than me. Millwall's problem is inherent, and it doesn't help if the chairman comes on and says it's a minority – they need to sort it out themselves, lead from the top and say that such behaviour will not be tolerated. I found it amazing that there was the occasional black face among their fans, and even black stewards – that is something I've never been able to work out. I was hit by coins and once, when I was receiving treatment for a cut from a clash of heads, missiles were landing all around me, so I said to the physio, Buster Footman, 'Patch me up quickly, I'm safer out on the pitch!' My only riposte was to score against them, and if I did, you would find me around the halfway line near the tunnel by the time ninety minutes came up.

We put that game behind us and continued our promotion push, but a poor March put paid to our automatic hopes. The nerves set in and we dropped as low as tenth, but we had a fantastic run-in, winning five in a row to scrape into the play-offs where we were up against Brentford, who had ended in fourth place. They were a good away side and despite our bombarding them they beat us 2–1 at Ashton Gate with Uriah Rennie in charge. The Bees beat us again by a single goal in the return. They bullied us into submission and I was gutted, being so close to promotion in my first season with the club, and now we would be a Division Two side for at least one more season. It was a real sickener because the play-offs also meant I had lost two weeks of our holiday time. To make things worse, Anita and I found ourselves on the way to Heathrow on a train full of Brentford fans on the way to the play-off final at Wembley. It reminded me of what might have been, and it was a miserable flight home to Bermuda. The only good thing was that Joe Jordan had left during the season and John Ward had come in – one of the best managers I was ever to play under.

CHAPTER SIX
A Tale of Two Cities

John Ward was like a breath of fresh air. He came in, and from our first meeting I knew he was going to help me progress and work on my game. When you are playing at the top level you need all the ingredients to succeed, but in the lower leagues many players need to be cajoled and require man-managing. A team that is almost relegated one year could be challenging for the title the next under a new boss, and it's all down to the players wanting to play for their manager and his belief in them.

A good manager will ensure that his team play to their strengths, even when the opposition is stronger, and will highlight the other team's weaknesses and concentrate on exploiting them. John Ward was excellent at looking after the players and making them feel good about themselves. I can hardly recall his tactical awareness – I just wanted to play football for him and give my all every game, something I thought I had been doing for other managers. But he knew how to get that little bit extra out of me and the other lads.

Ward's first words to me were, 'I know about what you do and how you play and I don't want you to change anything about your game. Just give me what you gave the club last year.' For me, that was a great start because I knew where I stood immediately. With that one sentence he gained my respect and I had a great desire to do well for him.

Out on the training pitches things improved beyond recognition. He would take the forwards to one side and say, 'Okay, let's do some finishing – show me what you've got', and I would think, 'I'm gonna impress him'. He would ask us to stick one in the top corner and as we did so he would say, 'That's not bad, but let's do better', always giving us little challenges to rise to. He was an understated but very effective manager. His assistant, former Leeds United striker Terry Connor, took us for extra finishing sessions and striker competitions so that we could concentrate on the job we were being paid to do.

Ward realised that there was no point in asking me to chest the ball down outside the box and then fire in a long-range effort – Shaun Goater doesn't score that type of goal! He worked on my sprints inside the box to get on the end of crosses, and generally worked on my strengths. There was also build-up play, designed for me to concentrate on the end result – picking the ball up outside the box, spinning off my man, flicking it around the corner, feeding the winger, then getting into position, and different interplays with my striker partners. This was what I needed; I knew my game was moving up a level. I watched highlights of games, saw goals I had scored as a direct result of the training we were doing, and it was altogether an exciting time because I could see how Ward and Connor were enhancing my game.

The team had belief and we were flying towards automatic promotion. We felt that every time we went out we would score goals and we had a saying among the strikers: 'Give us ninety minutes and we'll score you a goal.' It really didn't matter which one of us found the net – if it wasn't me, I was happy for Steve Torpey to score, or Kevin Nugent, or whoever was playing up front with me. If one of us was scoring, it kept the spotlight off the strike force and stopped the media focusing on us and adding extra pressure. If you are winning so much the better; the fans aren't bothered as long as the goals go in. But if you are losing, as a forward the focus tends to fall on your shoulders. If a partner was enduring a barren run I would say before a game that it was my job to help him score that day. If his confidence was low he would create fewer opportunities for me, so I was always aware that I needed a partner who was on his game – and if he wasn't, it was up to me to help him through it. I didn't like playing with players who had their own interests at heart, and I've had a few of those down the years.

I had been unselfish throughout my career and I had once been told at Manchester United that I was too nice in front of goal – but I played for the team because I came from an amateur environment where every man was equal and we were all fighting for the same cause. Back in Bermuda, if I had an opportunity to score but felt a teammate had an even better chance, I would pass it to him because I was playing for the team. I didn't arrive with the professional's attitude of 'I ain't passing to you because it's more important for me to score and if I fail, so be it', yet that was how some players thought.

John Ward brought in one or two new faces to bolster our bid for promotion in pre-season, and one of them was Shaun Taylor. He was an inspiration in our team. He never let the side down and was our Mr Dependable. He steadied the defence and was as solid as a rock, as well as being a terrific captain. Colin Cramb arrived at the club too. He had one or two nice moves in his locker and was a tricky forward who averaged maybe one goal every three or four games. He could lift the crowd, but would never score you twenty goals in a season. All the new players complemented those who had missed out in the previous season's play-offs, and we had a team determined to kick on and win promotion automatically. We ticked along well, and by February we knew that if we could put a decent run together for the last few months of the season we would have a really great chance of achieving our goal. I was finding the net on a regular basis and was very happy with life in Bristol. The fans seemed to like me, and it was reciprocal – I enjoyed great craic with my teammates and Anita and I were very happy at Nailsea.

I was voted in the PFA Division Two team of the season and the club offered me a new contract. I was very close to signing it – why wouldn't I have been? I didn't feel that I needed to move on because I loved playing under John Ward, so when March 1997 came around and Manchester City came in for me it really threw the proverbial spanner in the works. I had accepted in my heart that I would never play at the highest level and had settled on being the best I could at the level at which I was playing. I still had dreams and aspirations, but they were not all-consuming; I was happy with my lot and after eight years of earning a living in the bottom two divisions in English football I was just keeping things real. Then, completely out of the blue, City made their move for me.

After training one day John Ward came up to me and said, 'Man City are interested in you. Do you want to go?' It was about three days before the March deadline and I had not even thought about moving on. We were heading for Division One and that was all I was concentrating on. I remember seeing Manchester City fans going berserk with their players after they

57

had been relegated a few years earlier and had remarked to a Rotherham teammate, 'Their fans are crazy! I'd never play for them because they'd eat you alive'. But when the manager said 'Man City' the penny dropped and I realised what a huge club they were and that now they were interested in signing me. This was the club about which I used to wind up my old mate and diehard City fan, Ally Pickering. 'Who's Man City? I never heard of them', I would say to him.

I said to Ward, 'Yes, of course I'm interested!'

That was it for the time being. For a couple of days I heard nothing, and I thought it was never going to happen. Then, at 1pm on deadline day, my agent, Mark, called me to say the two clubs were trying to thrash out a deal.

It is standard to decline the first offer, which we did, even though to be quite honest I was more than happy to accept anything. Mark called again half an hour later to say everything was agreed. He gave my fax number to City and told me that they would call me within the next hour or so; all I had to do was sign the papers and return them so that the club could deliver them to the FA in time for the move to go through before the 5pm deadline.

I waited at home for what seemed like an eternity. It got to quarter to five, and still nothing. Then, to my relief, the phone rang, the fax clicked on and five pages of documents slowly came through. I signed the papers, dialled the number and tried to feed in the paperwork. My fax had jammed! Talk about timing! I was losing control, panicking and shouting, 'It's broken! I can't send it, sort it out, sort it out!' Anita pushed past me, telling me that she would do it – and she did, of course. She took a photo of me shortly afterwards, for posterity – because I was so stressed that the fax machine had very nearly scuppered that dream move. Of course, I could not know whether the club had sent through the forms to the FA before the deadline, and I was on tenterhooks for hours. The following morning I heard officially that I was now a Manchester City player – at a cost of £400,000. I had yet to speak with Joe Royle when club officials called me up to arrange my medical and a look around the facilities. I drove up to Manchester, and in my eagerness to get there received a speeding ticket – my first three points for the club!

Leaving Bristol was sad – I would have been happy to stay had it not been to move to a club like Manchester City. I had been presented with the chance to realise my boyhood dream by playing for a club with fine traditions and stature in the game. They might have been heading towards relegation from Division One, but this was my chance really to make some noise and I wasn't about to pass it up. Get those earplugs ready, Manchester . . .

CHAPTER SEVEN
Blue Murder

I had left a team where everyone was buzzing and full of confidence and joined a group of players who had no confidence whatsoever. Bristol City were heading towards promotion while Manchester City were in with a real chance of going down. Within a week of arriving at Maine Road all my confidence had evaporated, and that was mainly down to training at Platt Lane.

Because it was so accessible, adjacent to two roads with see-through fences, people would pull up in their cars and holler abuse at the squad. 'You're rubbish – you're not fit to wear the shirt', and suchlike. They either picked on individuals, or just had a general rant against the team. It was a dire situation for a team that was in need of encouragement. I became immersed in all the negativity. My prediction in the local press that I would score twenty-five goals a season was probably regarded as flippant, and no doubt wound up some of the fans, who must have been thinking, 'Who the hell is Shaun Goater anyway? Who's he played for? What's he ever done?' I had unwittingly made myself a target for a hostile crowd and my statement would add undue pressure during the coming months. I fully believed that I would score goals for City, but I should have kept my mouth shut and let my feet do the talking. You live and learn.

I had never played a game at Maine Road during my time at Rotherham or Bristol City and was unsure what to expect. I was happy to return to Manchester, but I had limited knowledge of the city, my original time there having been as an apprentice. Occasionally I would take the bus into town and I knew the immediate area around my Salford digs, but that was about it.

Joe Royle had brought Ian Bishop, a quality player, back to the club and we were both unveiled at the same press conference. After my medical – basic to say the least – I went with Ian to look around the stadium, and as I walked out of the tunnel and onto the pitch I thought, 'This is awesome!' This was the challenge I had yearned for, and I was determined to make the most of it.

During my first session I noted some of the players who were at the club and was amazed not only by the numbers in the squad, but by some of the quality players who were not in the team and were seemingly on their way out. Nigel Clough, an inspirational midfielder at Nottingham Forest, was one of them; and Georgi Kinkladze was still there but was not being played. There were others, such as Neil Heaney, who was neat and tidy on the ball but obviously was not delivering the goods when he played for the first team. I wondered why they were not producing for the manager, but could not work out what the problem was. There was already at least a team of quality players there. I was full of self-confidence, having done well with Bristol, and I just thought, 'Yeah, there are some top players here, but they ain't seen me yet – they haven't seen what I can do'.

Royle had made it clear that he was going to have a massive clear-out during the summer. There were between thirty-five and forty players in the squad, and he was of the mind that it was 'out with the old and in with the new', although he would have to reduce the wage bill before bringing in many more new faces.

I made my debut at Bradford City, and with just seven games to go we needed something from virtually every game. There were about 4,000 City fans present and they gave me a good reception. I thoroughly enjoyed the game despite our losing 2–1. I had at least two good chances, one a lob that bounced just the wrong side of the post, but I didn't score. I looked at the pluses and was pleased to have at least got in the right positions. The goals would come, I was sure of that, but City needed them to come *now*.

On Monday we returned for training to build ourselves up for the match with Stockport, but there always seemed to be someone shouting abuse at us from the fence, and I could see the effect it was having on the squad. I wondered how the club could even think about training in that location, and it was plain to see why they were struggling near the bottom of the league. The set-up was all wrong at Platt Lane; when Joe Royle later said he sometimes felt as if he were in a zoo when we trained, I knew exactly what he meant. It was an eye-opener, and made me realise that a strong mentality is needed to survive at the top level.

At Rotherham and Bristol City I had been a success so I had never had to deal with any mental challenges. The only challenges were the targets I set myself of beating the previous season's goal tally. Being barracked by the club's fans was a totally new experience.

There was a full house for my home debut against Stockport, and as I walked down the tunnel and heard the roar becoming louder and louder, then saw the crowd for the first time, the hair stood up on my neck and I felt shivers down my spine. As I neared the end of the tunnel I could see the first tier of the Kippax stand; a bit further on, and I could see the second tier, a few steps more and the third tier came into view, and while I was absorbing all this my mind shot back to my amateur days with North Village back home, running out onto those bobbly pitches in front of a handful of people. Then I zipped back to the present and thought, 'Yeah, this is the stage I want to play on'. There were about 32,000 people cheering and clapping as we ran out, and what an incredible feeling it was. The only other time I had got near this was at Wembley with Rotherham, so I was excited at the thought of having a cup final atmosphere every time I played a home match. I wanted to show these people what Shaun Goater could do and prove myself worthy of a club like Manchester City. I was buzzing, running on adrenalin as I loosened up. I knew I had scored a few against Stockport in the past and I was confident I could do it again. And I did – one of four we scored that evening in a 4–1 win. It was good to break my duck so early on, and we reckoned two more wins would probably be enough to save us from the drop.

We drew our next game 2–2 with Wolves, then lost 1–0 at home to Birmingham before losing at Middlesbrough by the same score. Kinkladze was out of the first-team picture at this point, and I was yet to play alongside him. I knew what he could do in training and he was a very special talent. We all knew the fans were desperate for him to play, but Joe did not want any passengers if we were up against it, and preferred a midfield scrapper in his team. It was already agreed that Kinky would go to Ajax, but Joe's decision not to play him put more pressure on the team because if a chance went begging or someone made a misplaced pass the fans would be thinking, 'Kinky wouldn't have missed that'. A win in any game would have made all the difference, but our final home game with QPR also ended without victory and we shot ourselves in the foot when Jamie Pollock and Martyn Margetson got in a terrible mix-up, and Jamie ended up heading the ball into his own net. We drew 2–2 (Kinky finally played and also scored) and were left needing a win from our final game at Stoke, and defeats for any two of the three teams above us. This seemed a possibility, because two of them were playing away. By half-time at Stoke, however, all three of the clubs above us were comfortably ahead and we were as good as down, despite leading our own game.

Looking back, I am not convinced that any of the teams whose help we needed were that bothered about Manchester City and whether or not we were relegated to Division Two for the first time. Some of them may even have thought it would be a good thing if we were not around to regroup and put in a promotion push next season. I say this because if I were involved in a game where I knew that losing would relegate Manchester United, I'm not sure how hard I would try! I think a lot of players that day must have been thinking, 'Hmm, Manchester City could go down if we don't win? Where's the catch?' and ultimately that told on the day. We won our game 5–2. I scored a couple of goals and then dislocated my shoulder after about seventy minutes and had to come off. I was still hopeful that things would work out for us. I had not heard a thing about the other games, and when I reached the doctor in the dressing room he said, 'Shaun, do you want the good news or the bad news?' I said he'd better give me the good news and he replied, 'Shaun, your shoulder is dislocated – the bad news is we're going to be relegated'. The pain in my shoulder suddenly became worse.

Despite playing for most of the season with Bristol City and learning they had won promotion, it meant more to me that I was part of a team that had been relegated within a few weeks of my arrival. I was devastated, and when Joe came in he just told us we had done all he had asked of us and there was nothing more that we could have done. He told us to go and rest, and come back next season to take the league by storm. The lads were understandably quiet as we reflected on what had happened, and on the coach back we spoke about anything other than the game. When we eventually did, it was about the three teams that had lost against the teams above us, and we were determined to give them all some payback if we ever got the chance.

A few days later my mate Greg Goodridge from Bristol City called and said, 'Hey, Goats, what's happening? We're going out and we want you to come down and get your mind off what's happened.' I said I would, but he should warn the others that I wasn't in the happiest frame of mind. It was good to see my old mates again; I was pleased for them because they were a terrific bunch with a great manager and excellent support. A few of the fans came up while we were out and said nice things, which lifted me briefly, but I left before the end of the evening and headed home. I just wasn't part of Bristol City any more and I felt a little out of place. A few people told me I had made the wrong decision in leaving, but I knew I hadn't. It was all about challenging myself at the next level, and being able to play in front of 30,000 fans every week was a dream come true. A couple of days later Anita and I were off to Bermuda for the summer and a well-earned rest. When I go home I relax and eat what I want. I love to barbecue and I invariably put on a few pounds before I return to work. I carried on regardless, despite Joe Royle's warning that he would fine anyone who gained 4 pounds or more a week's wages.

The only exercise I did back home was a spot of backyard football with the guys from North Village and Boulevard, over at Bernard's Park, and I had no intention of changing my routine. I knew I could lose the weight in pre-season and besides, I never gained a great deal. When I returned to Manchester for the weigh-in in July Joe Royle said, 'You're 12 pounds over, Shaun, and unless you lose 7 pounds in a week you're fined a week's wages'. I thought, 'What? I'm still lighter than most of the players at the club even with the extra weight on', but he wasn't messing around. My usual weight was around 11 stone 5 pounds, which is fairly light. Most of the other guys weighed in at around 13 stone. I said, 'You're kidding me! I'm 12 stone and you're gonna fine me?' My pocket was going to hurt!

The only other player up for a fine was Lee Crooks, who was a heavy guy anyway. He had to lose 4 pounds before the end of the week. I was still staying in a hotel at this time, the Copthorne by Old Trafford. 'How the hell can I lose that much weight eating hotel food?' I asked myself. The chef was a City fan and promised to help me, but he kept cooking some fancy meals, great food that I couldn't pass up, so I turned for a bit of advice to Jamie Pollock, who I knew was a very disciplined guy and always on top of his weight.

Jamie told me I needed to cut out this food and that food. 'Jamie', I said, 'once you say I can't eat something, I'm gonna eat it.' Even so, I began to eat salads for the first time in a bid to keep on top of things. Jamie advised me to do what he called a 'fat-burner run', which meant going for a ten to twelve minute run in the morning so I could jump on the scales at the club each morning knowing I had lost something. At times that was the will to live!

I would arrive for training, weigh in with my stomach grumbling, then go out for training. It wasn't ideal because pre-season training is designed to help you regain your fitness and can be pretty gruelling. By the end of the week I weighed in for the last time and had lost the required 7 pounds. Lee Crooks had also managed to lose the required amount. After training that day I ate everything – if there was food to be eaten, I was having it. I had been totally zapped of body fluids and energy, and I needed to get back to something like a normal diet. Joe told me I needed to lose another 4 pounds or so in the next few weeks and must then remain around that weight for the rest of the season, which I did.

Home life was getting better for Anita and me, with the money I was earning making a big difference in our lives. It had taken nine years to reach this point and it meant that we no longer had to look at finance to buy a car on credit. We could shop in the nicer stores and eat out whenever we wanted to. We weren't extravagant – we had spent too long just getting by to splash out – but it was nice to be in a position where we could choose. I was popular back home, but in my days at Rotherham and Bristol the wages had not matched the fame. I had been earning the same or less than most average workers in Bermuda, and it felt odd to have become famous on the island when financially I was no better off than anyone else.

We wanted to put roots down and began looking for a home in the Manchester area while I worked hard at training in preparation for my first full season at the club. Willie Donachie was a great coach. He would take us out for a run, saying 'Just stay with me', and then charge off into the distance! He was a fit guy, even at 50 or so, and left me thinking, 'Why do I always go to these clubs where the old guys are as fit as hell?' He had a saying, 'If you're behind me, you're bloody well cheating us!' and I used to think he must just be talking to me because I was always behind him. On one occasion when Willie had us doing running sessions I was within range of him for the first time. I wanted so badly to beat him; at that stage of the run he was usually half a lap in front of me, but now he was only 20 yards ahead. He might have been having an off-day, but I thought, 'I can beat him!' and as I closed up on him during the last lap I could almost hear him thinking, 'I'm not feeling the best today, but I'm not going to let Shaun beat me – I'll never feel that bad.' We were slogging it around the final lap, by now going at walking pace, and he held firm, kicked on and beat me by about 5 yards. I had just wanted to say that I had beaten him once, but I couldn't and I doubted I would ever get that close again. So what did he do? Congratulate me for my sterling effort in pushing him so hard? No, in between gasps he shouted, 'If you're behind me, you're cheating me!' I could feel his eyes piercing my body, but I could not have cared less – I was a spent force that day.

Other players in the squad had no such problems with running, and one of them was Paul Dickov. He was always among the leading pack and was just a naturally fit guy. Once, on a trip to Lanzarote, Joe told us to go out and let our hair down, so we did. We had a great night on the town and Ian Bishop, Danny Tiatto, Dicky and a few of the other lads had a few pints and really enjoyed themselves. I enjoyed myself too, but being a non-drinker I headed back to the hotel about midnight while the rest of the boys probably arrived at about 2 am. The next day we were at a training camp and Willie shouted, 'Right, we're just going to have a light session'. Of course, it was anything but light, but I thought that for once I'd show these lads a thing or two about fitness because they had had a heavy night. Who was out at the front? Paul Dickov.

Finally it was time to play a few friendly matches and gear up for the new season. I knew City fans had a reputation for following the club in numbers but had only had limited experience of it. Before kick-off – against a team I'd never even heard of – all the talk among the players was about how many City fans would be there. A few of the guys made guesses and then asked me how many I thought there would be. 'Oh, about 200,' I said, 'we're in the middle of nowhere'. We ran out and there were about 5,000 City fans all around the ground. I wondered where they had all come from. I had seen a sprinkling of shirts outside the ground on the way in, but had no idea quite how well supported we were around the country. We would be attacking, our fans were cheering us on; we would defend, and our fans were at the other end. The whole stadium was packed with our fans, and I reckoned there would be only a few other clubs capable of doing that. It made me realise what fantastic support we could utilise if we could get on a roll. From then on, when the lads asked me how many fans we would bring to a particular game, I would always go over the top and say, 'Oh, about 10,000! – No, seriously, only about 5,000'. Having that kind of backing made us feel good and gave us the confidence to think we could get out of Division Two at the first attempt. The fans may have been disappointed with where we were, but they still gave us such amazing backing, and our one thought as we approached the first game of the 1998/99 season was that we were going to repay their loyalty.

However, nobody, it is safe to say, had a clue about the dramas that lay ahead . . .

CHAPTER EIGHT

ScapeGoat?

A s we sat in the dressing room before our first league game of the season against Blackpool, we all knew we had to win promotion. Maine Road was full and although most people saw a club of our size in the Third Division as slightly surreal, that was exactly where we were and clubs would be queuing up to claim the bragging rights over us. Joe Royle had made clear what he expected of us in the coming months. Yet it was not until chairman David Bernstein popped in to see us towards the end of pre-season training a few weeks earlier that the penny really dropped as to what another season at this level could do to a club like Manchester City.

The chairman said, 'Look, lads, this is a vital time for the club and a critical era for us all. You could all be part of history because the club has never been this low; and you could all be part of restoring this club back to its rightful place in the Premiership.' As he spoke, I was believing it – yet not believing it.

Then it just hit us. I could see and understand his thinking, and looking ahead at the possible promotions we could be involved in, it all made sense. 'You could become legends', he added and I never forgot what he said, because he could have been talking just to me. Normally when a chairman comes in you switch off after a few seconds – but not this time. It was quite a speech, and it had a galvanising effect on all of us that day.

We knew we had the ability to fly right out of the Third Division. Our manager believed it, too; but initially we thought we would play our way out of the league. We thought from the start of the game that we would pass the ball around, create a chance and score – simple as that! Joe had warned us that teams would want to scrap for everything against us, kick us off the park if necessary, anything to get a result, and we expected that, but we were still in for a rude awakening. Every team treated the game as their cup final and in some ways fed off our own fans' edginess, growing in confidence if we didn't start our home games well. They could sense our nervousness and must have wondered whether we were as good as we had been made out to be. If they did take the lead, things became worse, our crowd grew more anxious and it became a vicious circle. Some of the sides we played would turn up, give perhaps one of the performances of their lives, and we would go away saying, 'How the hell did they just play the way they played?' For the majority of teams even a draw was a great result, and for the first half of the season we didn't know how to handle it. I remember losing 2–1 at Lincoln and watching the home fans run on to the pitch in their hundreds, as though they had just won the FA Cup final. That's when I realised what beating City meant for these sides.

We began well enough. I scored against Blackpool on the opening day and the 3–0 win was exactly what was expected.

There were 32,500 fans that day, which was not a surprise to me or any of the other lads. We just knew the supporters would be behind us, as they always were.

However, the next game, at Fulham, ended in a 3–0 defeat and we also lost one of our key defenders, Kakhaber Tskhadze, for the season with a serious knee injury. We beat Notts County 7–1 in the League Cup and I bagged a couple, then I scored a last-minute equaliser against the same team a few days later in a 1–1 draw. I recall our fans being fiery that day! I got another couple against Walsall and a late winner at Macclesfield, but despite a decent start to my first full season I had the feeling that the fans didn't particularly like me. I could not put my finger on it, but they just weren't taking to me and I could not work out why. Everywhere I had been I had scored goals and the fans loved me, but at City it was different, and it would take me all season to work out why. Did they believe I wasted a number of chances before I scored, or was it because of my confident claim of twenty-five goals per season when I had first signed? I don't know, but studying one of my teammates would eventually lead to a complete turnaround of opinion.

Our form was not good going into autumn, and Maine Road had become somewhere best avoided by the faint-hearted. Because there was so much anxiety and nervousness in the air, the management took the unusual step of stopping us warming up in front of our own fans. Willie Donachie's job was to ensure the players were not only fit and tactically aware, but also confident and mentally strong. Even warming up at Maine Road could dent the players' confidence, especially if boos were heard when certain names were announced. Willie arranged for us to start warming up at Claremont Road Primary School, about 100 yards from Maine Road. It was a highly unusual step to take, but one that our coach believed would benefit us in the long run.

It was a bizarre situation. We would get ready to warm up, then climb aboard a minibus and drive over to the school. Fans would hammer on the windows during the journey, shouting 'Come on!' and suchlike. We would arrive at the school, do our warm-up – sprints, passing and various other routines – and then board the minibus again and return to the ground.

The truth was we were more comfortable playing away. I thought training at the school was a great idea because it allowed you to start a match with a clean slate rather than hearing your name booed before a ball had even been kicked. There was nothing worse than hearing 'No. 9 – Shaun Goater – boo!' It probably confused the fans a little because every team warms up before a match – but we didn't any longer, and the first they saw of us was when we went out to start the game. We began to focus on the opposition once more, rather than on the fans, and I think it worked well. Whether the away team took heart at our unusual step I cannot say.

We were still drawing too many games, and one of them was at my old friends Millwall. I knew what to expect as a black player at Millwall, and I just blanked out the racial abuse I was getting – and always had done – but we took a point, and so long as I scored or helped prevent them win I was happy.

Every time I had the ball at my feet or challenged for it in the air, the Millwall fans made ape sounds. If I found myself near the touchline for whatever reason, I'd hear the shouts of 'you black b*****d'. It's not just the words that hurt. It was the threatening tone in their voices. Despite many of them being kids, it was real hatred. The police and stewards did not seem to have any control. The worst incident came just after our late equaliser through Lee Bradbury. We celebrated the goal naturally enough, and did nothing to intimidate or taunt the home fans, yet a mob of thirty or more came pouring onto the pitch and started heading towards us. Fortunately they turned back before they could reach us. But the message was clear enough: score another and we will do you. It sounds ridiculous but that is how worried we were.

We had a few indifferent results before I scored another late winner, this time at Wigan, to move into double figures for the season. We were still well off the pace at the top, and successive losses to Lincoln and Reading only made things worse. We were a ship without a rudder and there was no natural leader on the pitch to pick us up by the scruff of the neck and give us all the occasional shaking.

That was, until Andy Morrison arrived.

I had played against Andy a few times and had enjoyed our tussles because he was a big centre-half who would eat me up all day if the ball was in the air – but put it down the side of him instead of the channels and he couldn't catch me. We had a bit of banter, and I recall saying, 'Yeah, I've got a video of me celebrating a goal when you were supposed to be marking me.' Andy growled back, 'You know you never scored against me'. I said that a video didn't lie, to which he replied, 'You couldn't have done, because if you had, you wouldn't have been around to score another'.

Andy gave the team a big lift and we began to play – and win again – after he was signed from Huddersfield Town for £80,000. He knew what his role was and what he needed to do, and when he spoke, the lads listened. I think he responded to the fans too, and he was determined to lead us out of the Third Division. He had arrived with the tag of a hard man and I think he wanted to live up to that every time he went out on the pitch. Nobody messed with Andy: he was a terrific leader and he enjoyed the billing he had been given. You tend to want to hang on to a good tag, just like the 'Feed the Goat and he will score' chant that I suppose I earned at City in later seasons. I wanted to live up to that song, but the off-field persona didn't always match the one a player might project on the pitch – and Danny Tiatto was the perfect example.

Danny arrived at the club and was a quiet, unassuming guy. There was nothing aggressive about him whatsoever and he began his City career by being regarded as just a normal player. But somewhere down the line he showed his fiery side during a game, and when the fans saw that side of him they loved it and wanted more. Danny twigged, and began to live up to a hard-man image. It was a role he grew into and he effectively reinvented himself. So with players like Danny, Andy and Dicky in the side we had an edge to our game that we would need in the months ahead. The only trouble was that we were well down the table and almost half the season had gone. It was going to take a monumental effort to win promotion, and we would need a near faultless second half to the season to achieve our aim.

Our form began to improve steadily, but although we weren't losing many games we weren't winning that many, either. The pressure built as we slipped down the table and our habit of dropping points was now causing a sizeable gap between us and the leading pack. There were other concerns, too, that had a negative effect on the team. Just scraping a draw at Darlington in the FA Cup and then needing extra time to beat them in the replay was one of them, as was an embarrassing Autoglass Windscreens tie with Mansfield at Maine Road. We lost that, effectively ensuring that the morale at the club was at an all-time low.

Worse was to follow. I was injured for the trip to York City, but I travelled with the squad and sat in the stands. Watching your teammates instead of actually playing with them gives you a different perspective and I was amazed when Joe took Ian Bishop off. 'Oh, God', I thought, 'don't take Ian off – what are you doing? He's the one who gets us playing.' Bishop was our only really creative outlet; with him on the pitch you always felt there was a chance, but when he went off the City fans started chanting at Joe, 'You don't know what you're doing!' York went on to win 2–1 and we slipped into the bottom half of the table. Many fans recall this as the club's all-time low point and it proved to be something of a watershed for us. Ian was fed up on the coach home, saying he could not understand why he had been brought off when he felt he was controlling the game. Joe and the rest of us needed a win badly, and just after Christmas we won 1–0 at Wrexham. A few days later we were at home to Stoke City. If we were going to gather some momentum it was now or never.

Not 100 per cent match-fit, I was on the bench, and by half-time the crowd, who had come to really get behind us despite the way things were going, were baying for blood as we went in 1–0 down. Joe brought me and Danny Tiatto on at the break and something was definitely in the air as we ran out for the second half. The lads suddenly seemed to spark into action and Danny, Tony Vaughan and Dicky were firing the crowd up with some full-blooded, totally committed challenges. Then I ran out wide, back-heeled the ball inside, and from the cross Dicky equalised. Then we grabbed another through Gareth Taylor to win 2–1. The stadium was rocking and that game gave us the belief that we could still salvage our season.

We narrowly went out of the FA Cup at Wimbledon in the next game and then drew at Blackpool, but our confidence was definitely growing. Next up were Kevin Keegan's Fulham, who were the leaders at the time. If there was ever a time we needed to put on a decent show this was it. I went into the game thinking how much I would like to score against a team run by Keegan, a former England striker. I often had little incentives like that to keep myself on my toes – sometimes it would be an England goalkeeper I wanted to put one past, or an international centre-back whom I was up against. These were just little milestones I could collect during my career, and also something I could look back on in future years.

I wanted Keegan to remember me (how prophetic that would prove to be!), and for him to say, 'Yeah, I remember that game – that boy Goater ruined our day!' Games like that stick in my mind. I achieved my ambition by scoring in a 3–0 win – a great result for us.

We drew at Walsall and then travelled to Stoke where we won 1–0. It was live on Sky, and I remember Gerard Wiekens' goal really well because my best mate Kyle Lightbourne was marking him! I always spoke highly of Kyle and Bermuda football to the other lads and I told Gerard, who had become a great friend by this time, that my mate was going to terrorise him that day. Gerard said, 'He ain't got nothing for me, Shaun', and brushed off my warnings. Of course, it was Kyle who marked Gerard at the set-piece he scored from, and to this day Gerard says, 'So where's your Bermudian mate, then? I made a run for him, a run for me and the ball ends up in the back of the net – where was he?' I still get a lot of stick about that. Obviously I was really pleased with the win, but I knew I would never live down my talking up of Kyle. Whenever Gerard and Kyle talk now it is always the first topic of their conversation, Kyle saying, 'Yeah, but I was killing you all game – you were following me non-stop', and Gerard replying, 'But I scored'. And Kyle knows he can't top that.

I suppose I hit it off with Gerard because he and his wife Angelique were very similar to Anita and me. We both enjoyed quiet lifestyles and had similar personalities – the Dutch and Bermudian people both have a laid-back style, and we enjoyed each other's company.

For our promotion push Joe brought in Terry Cooke and Mark Robins – both former United players. Mark had been a youth-team colleague of mine at Old Trafford. I wondered whether he would expect me still to follow his advice of not passing to the new kid – because, being the new kid here, he was the threat now. We beat Millwall 3–0 at Maine Road – always a pleasure. But there were some disturbing crowd scenes among their fans that day. I recall them tearing out seats and trying to cause as much trouble as possible. None of the City players felt it would get completely out of control because the police and stewards seemed to be coping with the situation, but we were aware of something going on. I believe there was also some trouble outside the ground later.

I continued to do my best, but still felt that the fans did not think that much of me. I was scoring, but they still didn't seem to be taking to me. I would figure out why later on, but meanwhile it was time to open a new credit account against Burnley, and I scored my first City hat-trick in a 6–0 win at Turf Moor. I just couldn't help scoring against Burnley and would be really disappointed if I ever played them and did not find the net. I was up front with Gareth Taylor that day. I enjoyed playing alongside him because he took on most of the aerial balls and was good at giving me knock-downs and little lay-offs.

Winning by such a huge margin away sent out a message to the rest of the division, and we were approaching the business end of the season in great form. Yet the hat-trick had not quite won the fans over! Things were improving, compared with my first dozen games, but clearly I still had a lot of work to do. We were still dropping the odd clanger at home and our 2–1 defeat to Oldham virtually ensured that we would not go up automatically; but seven wins from the next eight meant we would almost certainly make the play-offs. We were finally playing football the way we were supposed to and had got to grips with life at this level. If they wanted to slog it out, we would slog it out with them, and if

At three months old with my mother.
(Author's collection)

With my mother on my first birthday.
(Author's collection)

The North Village Bantams Under-15 team when I was fourteen. In the back row on the far right is Albert Caisey. Second from the left in the front row is Clinton Caisey, and third from the right is David Bascome. (Author's collection)

Having a kick about while at high school in Orange County, New Jersey. (Author's collection)

Scoring in a World Cup Qualifier game against Jamaica in 1994. (Author's collection)

Proud to have signed for Manchester United. (Author's collection)

Returning to my former high school, Whitney Institute. The school renamed the gymnasium in my honour. (Author's collection)

World Cup Qualifiers vs El Salvador in their national stadium, 1992. (Author's collection)

I returned briefly to play for North Village Community Club in 1988 in the FA Cup Final. (Author's collection)

Pictured with John Wardle, Chairman of Manchester City Football Club, after the last game at Maine Road Stadium. (Author's collection)

With teammate Peter Schmeichel at Maine Road. It was my last game for Manchester City and Peter's last retirement game. (Author's collection)

My new family: Anita and me with our six-week-old twin daughters Amaya (left) and Anais (right). (Author's collection)

With my wife at Buckingham Palace after receiving my MBE from Her Majesty The Queen for Services to Developing Football in Bermuda. (Author's collection)

Celebrating with my Rotherham United teammates after our win against Shrewsbury Town FC in the Auto Windscreen Final in April 1996. I was the first Bermudian to grace Wembley Stadium. (Author's collection)

Above: *Celebrating being promoted to the Premiership for the second time. (Author's collection)*

Right: *A proud moment after being voted fans' Player of the Year at Manchester City 1999–2000. (Author's collection)*

Below: *I passed Gary Neville the ball before scoring past Fabien Barthez in the last-ever Derby at Maine Road to score my 99th and 100th Manchester City career goals. (Author's collection)*

Running out for the last time to all the cheers at Southend's Roots Hall Stadium. (Photograph courtesy of Dave Scriven)

My last time singing 'Feed the Goat' to the Southend faithful after securing the championship of League One. (Photograph courtesy of Dave Scriven)

Celebrating as Champions of League One with Kevin Maher (left) and Lee Bradbury during the Bermuda Bonanza Theme Day at Roots Hall Stadium. (Photograph courtesy of Dave Scriven)

they could not match that they didn't have anything else to offer, whereas we could click up another gear and play teams off the park. Fortunately we had not left it too late to save the season, and with the weather improving we were able to play a more attractive style of football more often.

We lost at home to Wycombe and then drew 2–2 at Bristol Rovers, where I got my usual warm reception. I also scored, which was my only way of reacting to any stick I received. I would look up, give their fans a smile and think, 'I'll show you, don't worry' – and it was nice when I did. It was the best answer I could give. The 4–0 win against York City took me to twenty for the season, a total I was pleased with but it was slightly short of my twenty-five-goal target and also down on my recent seasons at Bristol City and Rotherham. Still, we had secured our play-off spot and were now just three games from winning promotion. First, we had to see off Wigan Athletic over two legs, and it was in one of these games I ended up the centre of a hugely controversial moment – and Wigan fans haven't forgotten about it to this day.

CHAPTER NINE

The Incredibles!

The last two weeks of the 1998/99 season will stay with me as long as I live, as they will no doubt with all City fans. Quite simply, you could not have scripted the events of May 1999 as we chased promotion via the much-maligned play-offs. Having experienced defeat against Brentford just two years earlier I was determined I would not go through the same feelings of disappointment again, and if I had to miss two weeks of my summer holiday it had better be worth it. Gillingham, Wigan and Preston were the other teams who had made the play-offs and our final position in fifth place meant that we played Wigan. I was not that bothered about either Gillingham or Wigan, but was happy to avoid Preston because they were a very good side who came to our place and caused a lot of problems. In fact, they had already taken four points off us during the season.

The first leg at Springfield Park began in the worst possible way when Gerard Wiekens took a throw-in and Nicky Weaver misunderstood the situation, allowing Stuart Barlow to nip in and score within the first twenty seconds. I had taken my eye away, expecting the ball to be launched my way any moment, and the next thing I knew, the Wigan fans were celebrating. It was a disaster, and if we conceded another we would be in real trouble. But we had a great team spirit and our little gem Paul Dickov came up with a late equaliser to take us back to Maine Road level at 1–1.

The return leg was understandably an edgy affair. It was fairly even until Richard Edghill whipped in a cross from the right. As the ball bounced towards me at chest height I lunged forward just enough to edge the ball over the line for the opening goal of the night. I ran off towards the City fans, looking towards the linesman to check that he was not flagging for offside. Our fans went crazy, but as we celebrated the referee ran up to me and asked, 'That wasn't a handball was it?' He had given the goal and I couldn't believe he was asking me that question ten seconds later! As if I would have said 'yes', anyway.

The truth is, the ball never touched any part of my arm – but that didn't matter to the Wigan players and fans. Matt Jackson and another lad were going spare, claiming I had handled it. 'That was handball Shaun, and you know it!' Jackson shouted. 'That was no handball, believe me', I replied, but the actions and body language of him and a few of his teammates incited the Wigan fans, who clearly thought I had scored an illegal goal. If I had, I would (pardon the pun) hold my hand up willingly. Why wouldn't I? I have nothing to lose now. It might have looked as though I had scored illegally, but I just used my body to score and it went in from somewhere just above my hip. Not one of my usual clean strikes!

Wigan clearly felt a sense of injustice, particularly after they'd been denied what seemed to be a clearcut penalty for a foul on

Kevin Sharp. Graham Jones crashed a late header against our bar –
but we held out to win 1–0 and book our place at Wembley. The
City fans poured on to the pitch within seconds, and before I knew
it I was being stripped of my kit and couldn't breathe as fans
mobbed around me. It was the scariest thing I have ever experienced because I was so exhausted and couldn't fend anyone off.
My arms and legs were being pulled around, people were grabbing,
hugging and kissing me, but I was struggling to breathe and when I
was gradually pulled over towards the tunnel I had lost a boot and
my shorts were halfway down my legs! I didn't care – I was just
happy to be able to move freely again and catch my breath.

If anyone had been in doubt as to what this meant for the City
fans, they weren't any longer, and each of us thought that there
was no way we could lose the final if this was their reaction to our
winning the semi-final. In the dressing room Joe said, 'That's what
it means to them and that's the expectation you have to live up
to'. He added that we had not won a thing yet and we should go
and rest up for a few days, let our bodies relax and then prepare
for the play-off final at Wembley – my second appearance at the
famous old stadium. Gillingham had seen off Preston and they
were now all that stood between us and a successful climax to a
dramatic season. But nobody had any idea of just how breathtaking the final would be.

We prepared for the game by keeping to our usual routine, and
stayed in a fairly average London hotel – nothing too expensive,
that was for sure. The big day arrived and all our families came to
the game. Anita was there, and my agent Mark with his son Sam.
We left the hotel and I got into my own zone, thinking about my
role and the game ahead. Then we began to see the City fans
along the route – and they just seemed to be everywhere. Next
thing we were pulling up at Wembley, just a few hours from kick-
off. We checked out the dressing rooms and took a walk out onto

the pitch. It was a grey, drizzly day but I looked around and the City fans were all gathered around the tunnel as we walked out, and it seemed as if three-quarters of the ground were our supporters. It was a fantastic feeling to see that kind of backing. My mind flashed back to my days back home, kicking a ball around the park, dreaming of playing an FA Cup final at Wembley, and here I was again for the second time in three years. The only thing I had learned from my previous experience of playing at Wembley was how sapping the pitch could be and how pre-match nerves and adrenalin could drain your energy away.

I would approach this game differently, to conserve energy for the later stages of the game, and I would later be glad that I had. I did not want to lose a game at Wembley, and although I had won a trophy there with Rotherham, this was a bigger stage – and a much bigger crowd, too.

The game itself reminded me of an evenly contested boxing match, both sides slugging away at each other and neither ahead on points. Early on Andy Morrison had to go off injured and Ian Bishop came on. Wembley is perfect for a player of Bish's quality, and he got us playing in the way he always did. It was evenly matched throughout and seemed to be heading towards half an hour of extra time. Then we entered the last ten minutes – and disaster. First Robert Taylor put Gillingham 1–0 up and then, around five minutes later, Carl Asaba made it 2–0.

Our promotion dream was in bits and I was thinking, 'Hell, ref, blow the whistle'. I had had enough, and I learned later that thousands of City fans had too. Some of them had even got as far as the tube. We figured this just wasn't happening for us and wanted an end to the pain. You get days like that in football, where you try everything but it just doesn't come off, but Gillingham were playing above themselves and we could not really complain about being behind.

As I was thinking like this the ball fell to Kevin Horlock, who drilled it home to make it 2–1 and two or three of us then ran into the net to retrieve the ball. As we jogged back to the centre circle we heard our fans begin to roar and get behind us again. I glanced over to the bench to see what the cheers were for and could see the fourth official holding up a board displaying five minutes of injury time. At that point, five minutes felt like half an hour and I thought, 'We can pull this back'.

Our fans were going crazy, shouting encouragement, and we could suddenly sense the Gillingham players' edginess and see it on their faces. We threw everything at them and were determined to make them pay for all the high fives they had given each other during the substitutions and the congratulatory pats on the back that suggested – understandably – that they had the game won. We pressed constantly.

The five minutes was just about up when the ball fell to me and I took a swing at it, but the defender made a fantastic block tackle and the ball deflected right into Dicky's path. He gave it all he had – taking the slightest of deflections, I think. It felt like slow motion as we watched the ball rocket past Vince Bartram in goal and into the back of the net. That's when the roar hit us and shook the stadium to its foundations. I thought, 'That's my little gem!'

After the game I told Dicky that I had meant that pass and said 'Paul, you know I saw you, don't you?' After he had scored, I had nothing left in my legs, but I still chased him! The celebrations were ecstatic and the comeback was nothing short of a miracle. The whistle blew; the Gillingham players looked as though they were in shock. If I could have placed a bet there and then, I would have put my house on us finishing the job in extra time because, so far as I was concerned, there was no way the game was going to penalties. We pressed forward to no avail and they hung on and took it to spot kicks. Even then, I thought this was a done deal.

Our comeback had been too dramatic for our name not be etched on the play-off final trophy.

Kevin Horlock stepped up to take our first penalty – he later told me that as he walked up to the ball the goal looked huge, but when he actually got to the spot he could not even see it any more! He put the ball down, tried to remain calm and thought, 'I know where I'm going to put it – to the keeper's right.' Then, as he looked up he thought, 'No, I'm going to put it to his left', but as he stepped back, he thought, 'To hell with it, I'm going to blast it!' But as he ran up he was still unsure, so he just hammered the ball as hard as he could and as he saw it hit the back of the net, he thought 'Thank f*** for that!' We all did.

We were all on the halfway line with our arms around each other and I was thinking that we had needed to do that. Then Weaves saved one and it was Dicky's turn. He ran up, and we watched in horror as the ball hit one post, rolled along the line, hit the other post and then out again! The thing was, he could have missed three penalties in a row after scoring that goal and it would have been a case of 'It's all right, Paul! Don't worry about it.'

Then Terry Cooke scored to make it 2–1 but Gillingham pulled one back with their next attempt. Richard Edghill's penalty was unstoppable, hitting the post and stanchion and bouncing high into the back of the net – it was a perfect penalty and made it 3–1. He grabbed the badge and kissed it and I was really pleased for him because he had had a bit of stick over the last few years, but he always did his best and never complained.

Gillingham took their fourth penalty at 3–1 down and I thought, 'Save this bloody penalty, Weaves'. He did just that, somehow saving it with his legs as he went the wrong way – he later said he had realised I was the fifth penalty taker and so had to save it or we had no chance. It would have been great to step up and score the winning goal, but the truth is, I could live without it.

We had done it, and had won promotion. We chased Nick and piled on top of him, and we just went nuts and celebrated, with the fans waving flags, joining in songs and wearing silly wigs.

From the low point of losing at York City and struggling in the first half of the season as every side we came up against treated us as a cup final – to this. What a great way to finish the season! And it was so important that we did it at the first attempt because it would have been really hard, mentally, to have to come back the next season and do it all again.

Afterwards I recall going back to the dressing rooms and popping into the Gillingham side and just saying, 'Unlucky, lads' – not with any malice, just to commiserate with them. But even as I opened their door, I could feel a vibe of depression envelop me. It was sapping, and I will never forget that feeling of what it must have been like to lose a game like that, because I felt it moment-arily as though it was me on the losing side. In theory, perhaps it should have been us, because we had no right to have come back from 2–0 down with a minute of normal time to go. We swapped shirts with many of the Gills lads and we later found out that some of them had sold them on, no doubt back to City fans. It didn't bother me and I still have my Gillingham shirt as a memento.

The nearby hotel where we were staying was full of City fans and the atmosphere was electric. We were so happy that we didn't even mind losing two weeks of our summer holiday – we just felt like 'When do we start again?' We were buzzing and eager to get going again, but Joe Royle just said, 'Well done, you put in a great effort for the club and you deserve all the praise you get. Now go away, have a good rest and I'll see you in July.'

I went home and everybody congratulated me on our achieve-ment. I had a great summer, relaxed and thoroughly enjoyed myself – but this time I watched my weight!

CHAPTER TEN

From Zero to Hero

Despite finishing as top scorer with twenty-one goals in season 1998/99, I began the following season feeling that my relationship with the City fans still had not improved. 'What have I got to do to impress these guys?' I asked myself. I had been top scorer in my first full season at the club but the odd jeer when my name was mentioned was evidence that, in their eyes, I still was not doing enough.

It was an odd situation. Was it because I had failed to fulfil my pre-signing declaration that I was good for twenty-five goals per season? I doubted it, but it did cross my mind. What was more confusing was the adulation heaped on the shoulders of my mate Paul Dickov. Dicky had finished with sixteen goals, and although he had been with the club a while longer than me, the only difference between us that I could see was his all-out effort and refusal to give up a lost cause. Then it clicked. I had to take aspects of Dicky's game and work them into mine. If the City fans liked to see their forwards closing down defenders and generally making life tough for them, I was up for that. I began to study Paul's style during matches. The ball would go to a full-back and he would race after him. The full-back played it inside to the centre-back and Dicky raced after him, inevitably forcing him into a hurried clearance or, if he hung on too long, he would be on the end of a clattering challenge. The fans loved it, and he had a knack of getting them off their seats and roaring the team on. He was like a rash; he would chase balls that were going out and he had no right to reach, and generally used his boundless energy to the benefit of the team.

Some days Dicky would arrive at the ground at the same time as me. He would look over and say, 'Let's get into this lot today'.

So while my game was totally different and mainly based on scoring or creating goals, I began to change the way I played, and when the ball was with defenders near me I would start chasing them down and generally adopt Dicky's methods. It would take a few months, but gradually I felt the fans begin to warm towards me. The goals were still going in, but now, in their eyes, I was contributing much more – and City fans love a trier! I was starting to feel at home and the tide was definitely turning.

During the summer Joe Royle had brought in Mark Kennedy, a talented left-sided midfielder. I didn't know much about Mark, but I knew that I could adapt my game to his so that he would still be playing to his strengths and I would also be playing to mine. That way we could get the best out of each other. He was a quality player who had played for Liverpool and was an Irish international. From the first few training sessions alone I saw he could go across players quite easily. 'I can work with this!' I thought. Danny Granville arrived also, and with the confidence we had gained from the play-off final we were buzzing and eager to start the new season. The supporters had their expectations, which I doubt will ever be lacking, no matter how well the club are doing or where they are in the league. As I write this, the expectation is to get a UEFA Cup place. When that is achieved it will be the Champions' League, and after that, can they win the Champions' League? It is natural to think that way, and good too, because it keeps you on your toes. In my early days at the club I thought that if we won a particular game or ended in a decent position in the table the supporters would be happy – no chance! Finishing ninth in the Premiership was a decent achievement, but the fans felt we should be in Europe, and that is what helped me to become a success at City: knowing that we would never be allowed by our fans to feel comfortable. I always had another level to reach or a challenge to meet, and I was desperate to succeed and achieve my goals.

We lost the opening game 1–0 to Wolves at Maine Road and knew that we would have to pick our game up; we could not allow one defeat to become two, or even three, because the pressure would start to build. We needed to keep our heads high and our confidence levels topped up. I opened my season account against Burnley (who else?), beating them 5–0 in the League Cup, and we followed that up with a 0–0 draw at Fulham, then beat Sheffield United 6–0 – exactly the reaction to the Wolves' defeat that we had needed.

Mark Kennedy scored the only goal in our win at Bolton – a 30-yard screamer – and I noticed that he could generate an enormous amount of power in his shots or crosses. Sometimes he hit a cross in so fast that you had to be right on the money or had no chance of connecting with it. We were beginning to take off, and realised pretty quickly that there was nothing for us to fear in this division. I was scoring, but most of my goals were the results of pouncing on mistakes from defenders, or anticipating where the ball was going to be. No one was providing killer passes and the only man capable of doing that was Ian Bishop, and he used to sit deep, just in front of the defence. Kennedy was not setting up many goals for me, partly because of the power of his crosses. Even at three-quarter strength he would send the ball flashing across the box like a heat-seeking missile.

It was nice to bag a couple at Southampton in the League Cup; they were a Premiership side and I was eager to test myself against better defenders. We lost 4–3, but my tally of seven in eight games was pleasing, and further proof that when the pitches are good and the sun is shining, the Goat likes to feed!

It was around this time that a young player from the youth team began to make the odd appearance here and there. Known by all back then as 'Ian Wright's boy', Shaun Wright-Phillips had arrived. In later years he would call the commentators before a Sky game and ask them to refer to him as Shaun Wright-Phillips rather than 'Shaun Wright' – he didn't want to ride on his father's reputation, and that was part of his coming of age and establishing his own identity – which of course he did eventually. So much so, in fact, that some referred to Ian Wright as Shaun Wright-Phillips' dad! He was an honest, hard-working lad, willing to learn, and at that point he was just finding his way. Soon after I got to know him he asked my advice about whether he should play for Jamaica rather than England in the future. I told him to keep his options open in case England came calling – which they did.

Back in the league we went to leaders Charlton and my goal helped us win 1–0, a good win for us because we had beaten the best the division had to offer. I could feel the majority of the fans were now with me; there was a definite warmth from them. Scoring goals, putting myself about when I didn't have the ball and my improved all-round play were doing the trick.

Things were going well and Joe signed Robert Taylor – whose goal had almost cost us promotion in the play-off final several months earlier – from Gillingham for fairly big money. I could sense that the supporters were pleased with the signing because he was a big, powerful lad who was adored by the Gillingham fans. I was concerned he had been brought in to replace me. Another striker, Lee Peacock, had also arrived, but I knew I had no problem with him. Within a few days he came into the dressing room and said, 'When do the lads go out?' from which I could tell that he was at City for a good time. It was bizarre because I had come thousands of miles to make a career here and there were lads – not necessarily Lee – who arrived at a big club, thought they had made it and were happy with their lot. But there was so much more hard work to do and if anything, this was when the real hard work began.

Taylor knew a lot about City – more than I did, in fact – and he had only just arrived. He knew about the club's history, the nationwide fan base and the right things to say, and he was quiet and respectful in interviews, not boasting about how many goals he would score. The fans seemed to take to him straight away, but I saw him as the first line of competition. I knew his goal ratio was pretty decent, although not as good as mine, yet the fans already seemed to believe in him – and when you have the fans behind you, you can really hit the ground running. I doubted whether Joe planned to play us both up front. One Taylor arriving was the signal for another to depart, and Gareth Taylor moved on to pastures new. There were no big names in the team. We all got along well and went to various functions as a team and Gareth was part of it all. I actually liked playing alongside him. He was honest, and I felt he was never really appreciated for the role he played at City.

Despite the added pressure I continued to find the net and kept my place in the team, and one of my goals was against Leeds in the FA Cup. It was nice to put one past Nigel Martyn, then an England keeper; I enjoyed scoring against players of that calibre – when I'm old and grey, I shall be able to tell people, 'Yeah, I scored against him!' We eventually lost that game 5–2. Lee Bowyer was exceptional for Leeds at the time and he destroyed us that day, scoring a fantastic half-volley.

Fulham were next up, and there was a big buzz about them at the time. Mohamed Al-Fayed was putting in a fair bit of money and Kevin Keegan was still their manager, ensuring that they played an exciting brand of football. They were then near the top, and possibly favourites to win the game, even at Maine Road. I had scored against them in Division Two and I wanted to leave my mark and make sure Keegan remembered me – and I think he did, because I scored a hat-trick in a 4–0 win. Chris Coleman was sent off in that game; I loved playing against him because he was a big defender I knew I could run around because he was not that mobile, and although he got the better of me in the odd game, overall I think I edged our battles. It proved we were getting things together at City; the fans were singing my name and it was great to hear them. Now I knew they accepted and were appreciating what I was doing; from now on there was no looking back.

A couple more wins over Nottingham Forest and Norwich respectively kept things rolling, but we then had an inexplicably long winless run that threatened to derail our promotion drive – a win over West Bromwich was our first success in seven games. We returned to winning ways and there was a nice surprise in store for me when we travelled to Grimsby Town. It was the first time I had captained City, although I was unsure whether or not I would be doing so until just before the game. Jamie Pollock was injured and I had seen a few reports that I might be called on to lead the team out, and that it would be a nice gesture because I had ridden the hard times and was now a popular member of the squad. As Joe called out the team sheet before the game he said, 'And the captain's going to be Shaun'. All the lads cheered. I felt very proud – and a little nervous.

My preparation before a game was all about me. I didn't have systematic superstitions such as tying my right bootlace first, but I did enter my own zone before kick-off and I could not really do that as captain! I wondered what to do, and then I realised, 'You know what? You've just got to be yourself.' I went around the lads saying, 'Come on lads, let's do it today!' but pretty soon I found I was out of motivational encouragement and could think of nothing else to say! Being one of the quiet ones, I was not used to all this geeing up. For a minute or so everything went quiet, so I started again, 'Come on, we can do this today!' I certainly wasn't an Andy Morrison type of skipper. I enjoyed my day with the armband, even though we only drew 1–1, and I kept it for several games in Pollock's absence. When the fans began singing 'One Shaun Goater! There's only one Shaun Goater', it was a proud moment, because I knew I'd turned things around. Things had come such a long way from the days when Joe read out the team sheet and I hoped, 'Don't pick me again, don't pick me again'. 'Shaun, you're up front', he would say, and I would wonder why he stuck by me through thick and thin. He believed in me, and I owe it to him for not bowing to crowd pressure and for believing I would win the fans over.

I really cannot remember when I first heard the song 'Feed the Goat and he will score', but I loved it. I recall the lads coming in at half-time and saying, 'Did you hear that song, Goat? They're singing about you', and it just caught on. Some people maintain it was during the 4–0 win over Fulham, others during the away win at Forest. I don't know who thought it up, but I definitely owe them one. The fans would sing when I scored, and if I didn't find the net I would put in a few strong challenges and they would start up again. I really wanted to keep that song going! Even Joe Royle would shout 'Feed the Goat!' during training, and in some ways it helped me become better known as a player. *Soccer AM* tried to get me on the show for a game called 'Feed the Goat' in which fans were taken out of the studio and attempted to kick as many balls as possible through a giant cardboard goat's mouth in the space of a minute to the background music of 'Feed the Goat and he will score'. I never took up the invitation, despite being asked a few times, because I was not very comfortable with being on TV and I preferred to keep a low profile away from the pitch. The song would play a huge part in my career; it became known up and down the country and I understand that it is one of the most popular terrace chants of recent times. I remember the Birmingham fans once singing 'Feed the Horse' for Geoff Horsfield, but it didn't have the same ring to it . . .

Fortunately all this was happening at a great time for the club, so I could enjoy it all the more. We had reached the last two games of the season, our penultimate game being at home to Birmingham City. We knew that if we got four points from the two games we would be promoted automatically. Charlton were already up and it was between us and Ipswich for the second spot. We played Birmingham on a Friday night, the game being broadcast live on Sky, and Ipswich were at Charlton the following day. When Robert Taylor scored the only goal of the night our fans went wild, and on the final whistle thousands poured on to the pitch, thinking we were as good as up. I remembered the feeling of being choked after we had beaten Wigan a year earlier to go to Wembley, and this time I sprinted off! A few fans caught up with me, but this time I was a lot quicker. Nicky Weaver was not so lucky; he was almost engulfed by the hundreds of well-wishers surrounding him. While the fans celebrated I thought, 'This isn't over yet', and sure enough Ipswich, no doubt fuelled by our victory scenes at Maine Road, won comfortably the next day at the previously impregnable Valley.

That meant we had to get something from our last game at Blackburn, and what an incredible game that would turn out to be – in fact, surreal would be a better description. Our supporters were everywhere, even on a hill overlooking the stadium, and when we ran out at Ewood Park it felt like a home game. Blackburn manager Graeme Souness had said that Charlton secured the title at Ewood Park two weeks earlier, and he didn't want to see another team celebrating in his own backyard. Those words must have worked because Blackburn were all over us in the first half. They hit the crossbar, they hit Nicky Weaver, one post, then the other – everything – and although they did find the net eventually they were only 1–0 up at the break. All the time they were killing us. 'I just want one chance – one opportunity', I thought. That was all I asked for.

During the interval Joe told us, 'If you want to lose and throw away all you've done over the season, keep playing the way you are because that's exactly what you're going to do'. Then he added, 'Go out there and play like you want to win this, like you want promotion, like it means something. You're waiting on them to do something so you can react but the good news is, you're playing sh** but you're only 1–0 down. You've got forty-five minutes to decide whether you want to be in this division or to play with the big boys. Now go out and show me what you've got.'

We sat there and thought about it for a moment, then ran out again for the second half. Dicky and I had not done much so we decided to really get into it, and within a few minutes Kevin Horlock put in the perfect cross and I knew it was coming to me. I thought about smashing my foot through it, but knew getting it on target was the most important thing, so I just decided to side-foot the ball. Fortunately the connection was sweet and it flew into the net. I ran off towards the Rovers fans with my hand to my ear – I could no longer hear them giving me any stick – I enjoyed that! City fans were jumping up all over the ground, and not too long afterwards Christian Dailly headed a long clearance past his own keeper to make it 2–1. Then Kennedy made it three, before Dicky added a fourth. That was it, and when the whistle went for full time I was thinking about all the chances they had had and failed to take. Blackburn's players were holding their heads in their hands, probably wondering how the hell they had lost the game, but for me it was destiny – no other explanation would wash.

Two promotions in two seasons – we went back to the dressing room, too exhausted to do anything and certainly with no energy to jump up and down in celebration. In fact, a couple of the pictures taken at the time show Dicky, Mark Kennedy and me sitting down, happy but completely whacked.

When we came out to greet the fans from the Ewood Park directors' box it was like being back at Maine Road. The whole pitch, bathed in sunshine, was a sea of City supporters waving flags, singing songs and jumping up and down – it was a fantastic sight, a moment when I wanted to freeze time, to savour the feeling for ever.

It was great to see the likes of Asa Hartford, Willie Donachie and Joe Royle sipping champagne afterwards – and being drenched in it by the lads – and to watch them thoroughly enjoy it. They had earned it with all their hard work.

I had a flashback to David Bernstein's words before our first Division Two game a couple of years earlier, and how he had said we could be legends. Although we were not legends as such, he was right in terms of our all being part of something special. Certainly at that point I had no thoughts about becoming a legendary figure among the City fans. The champagne was flowing, but I didn't need it to enjoy myself and I doubt I could have felt any happier.

I had also had some amazing news of my own a few months earlier – I was going to be a daddy, not to just one baby, but two.

Earlier in the year we had learned that Anita was having twin girls. But our dramatic game at Ewood Park almost turned into a disaster. While watching our win at Blackburn Anita had become far too excited. We were concerned she might be having a miscarriage and I took her to the hospital for tests. As there was a promotion party dinner at the Midland Hotel the day after the Blackburn win, I went along with Kyle Lightbourne, but didn't stay too long. Those forty-eight hours were a mixture of excitement and dread because we weren't sure whether our girls would be okay, but the doctor came in and told us everything was fine – the heartbeats were normal. But within those two days I had experienced every emotion imaginable.

Shortly afterwards Anita was allowed home, and a couple of weeks later we flew to Bermuda and then went on holiday to the Bahamas with Kyle and his wife Rosemarie. An awful lot had happened in the last year and the break was desperately needed. As I lay on the beach at Atlantis I thought about finally making it to the Premiership. It might have taken eleven years of hard graft and proving people wrong, but I had made it. It had been a fantastic season. We'd been promoted, I'd been voted City fans' Player of the Year and got into the PFA Divisional Team for the season. Now I could test myself against the best – little old Goat from the tiny island of Bermuda, population 60,000. I couldn't wait to get started . . .

CHAPTER ELEVEN

Proving a Point

I will never forget 21 June 2000 because that was when the government of Bermuda decided to honour me with a whole day of my own. For twenty-four hours the day became officially known as Shaun Goater Day in accordance with the declaration made by the Premier Jennifer Smith. A motorcade was arranged for me. It began at my mother's house on North Shore Road and travelled to my old primary school, Victor Scott School, before moving down Pond Hill, along Court Street to the Premier's office and back to City Hall. The school even broke off to allow the kids to come out and wave to me – a great feeling, even though a few lads were playing football instead of waving. I had to smile because I knew that was exactly what I would have done!

All my family were at City Hall – my mum, stepfather, aunt Idae Mae, uncle Clyde and one or two cousins. The Mayor William Frith and a few dignitaries were in attendance, among them the Minister of Sport Dennis Lister.

Several speeches were made and I got up to say a few words and thank people like North Village Community Club, Mark Trott, Andrew Bascome and everyone who had helped me in my early years. After that a lunch was put on at the Hamilton Princess Hotel to which all my friends and family were invited. It was great to see people like Harold Dock Dowling and the Bascome brothers there. It was an emotional time for me, and I ended up crying as the various speeches were made. My aunt Idae Mae told me, 'Every day is a Goater day', but it was a really marvellous occasion and I shall never forget it. I was also invited to open a VIP area at the airport when we first arrived home, so I felt very honoured and privileged.

I had sustained a knee injury after our victory at Blackburn in May and felt I needed an operation to cure it, but was advised by our medical staff that rest might do the trick. However, this didn't work and it cost me the start of the season.

There had been no new strikers signed by the club during my absence and I returned to pre-season training at Carrington expecting to start up front for our opening 2000/1 fixture at Charlton Athletic. By the first week of August, however, Joe had brought two big-name forwards to the club and I knew I had hard work ahead in pre-season to earn my place in the opening match. First to arrive was former World Footballer of the Year George Weah, and a week later Paulo Wanchope was signed for £3.75m – a club record.

It was good for me to watch, and to see what these players produced in terms of goals. Their arrival was also a sign of the club attempting to make some noise in the Premiership. They were investing a lot of money in these players and I was keen to see what they could do. In Paulo's case you never knew what he was going to do next, but I found as time went on he was fairly predictable because whenever there was something easy to do, he would do the opposite.

I liked playing alongside him because he was like a typical Bermudian forward in that he liked the flicks around the corner, the dummies, and though he looked gangly he was actually always in control of the ball. He just looked ungainly because he had a kind of lolloping stride – almost giraffe-like! He was tall and strong, and he could lay the ball off and hold up play well.

I had always considered myself a good judge of players and the truth is you are only as good as the players around you – I really believe that – so I was never under the impression that these players would come in and score twenty goals a season. I knew how I had scored most of my goals the previous season, and the supply lines were not likely to change. With the exception of the assists from Kevin Horlock – I had been assisted perhaps three times each by Kennedy, Bishop and Terry Cooke – most of my goals had simply been the result of being in the right place at the right time. Paulo had the ability to make a few goals out of nothing, but George was 33 and was not going to start beating five players and slamming it home from 30 yards – he would rely on a good supply line, and though he was a legend in football I was not worried about his arrival. In time I would be proved right.

One of George's jobs would be to lay the ball off and attract a lot of attention so that other players could score. There would be times he would get to the byeline, then chip balls back to the edge of the box, probably expecting someone to run in and volley it into the top corner, but I just thought, 'George, you ain't at AC Milan any more!' George was a couple of levels above us all in terms of ability and I looked forward to observing that when I learned that he had signed. Early on I picked up an injury that would keep me out for quite a few games and George, having seen me play in a few pre-season matches, paid me a massive compliment, asking 'When are you back?' Maybe he knew I had a knack for reading certain situations in and around the box, but even though I would never actually play with him in a competitive game during his short time with the club I took it as a big pat on the back.

George was very much as I am today – wanting to pass on information and help coach the youngsters if they were willing to hear what he had to say. In fact, the only time I felt slightly envious of Shaun Wright-Phillips was when George asked him to stay after training had finished to mess about around the goals and pass on various tips and observations. I felt this was just for Shaun because he was a kid and I would watch as they did various moves and tricks. I watched from the side, although I was desperate for him to pass on some of his vast experience and knowledge to me, but he never chose to do that, to my regret.

Having been ruled out for the first five weeks with the knee injury – further aggravated in a pre-season friendly against Linfield at Windsor Park – I watched the early matches from the sidelines. I wondered why Joe used Ian Bishop so sparingly, because he was such a positive influence on the team and could control a game. The preferred combination seemed to be Jeff Whitley and Alfie Haaland – a grafting midfield rather than a creative one. They could break up play well, but neither of them could really provide the killer ball. Alfie had arrived from Leeds with a lofty reputation, but I did not see him as anything special or any different from the players we already had at the club – he was another Jeff Whitley, and, being from Leeds, he just had a bigger profile, but that's management for you. Joe obviously saw something in him that he liked, and that was that. Steve Howey was another big-name signing who had been bought to bolster the defence. Steve was a big signing for the players as well as for the club. When somebody has established himself for a team like Newcastle you know he can play. He knew about the big games and the expectation of playing for a big club. Steve got on well with Ian Bishop and a couple of the other lads to form a little booze crew, all of whom enjoyed a drink at the time. When we went out they would be around for most of the night, but when it came to about 11 pm they would disappear and I would think, 'There goes the crew!'

A dozen games passed – the longest absence I had had during my time in England – before my knee problem cleared. That allowed Wanchope and Weah to start the campaign pretty much unchallenged. Our opening game was at The Valley against the side who had come up automatically with us the season before. With Charlton's limp display against Ipswich almost costing us a place in the Premiership the previous season, we felt we owed them one, but we wound up on the wrong end of a 4–0 defeat as they rediscovered their appetite for winning. Paulo scored a hat-trick in the next game against Sunderland and was out of the blocks and running, but just nine games later George Weah quit City.

It was during the visit of Bradford City that George had his last involvement with the club, barely two months after signing. I was fit enough for a place on the bench – and what a proud moment this match would be for me. I was substitute alongside Ian Bishop, Kevin Horlock, Tommy Wright and George and after about fifteen minutes the crowd began singing 'Feed the Goat' – I will never forget that, ever. I ran down into the corner, warming up, and there was a loud cheer. I wondered what George Weah made of it. Here was one of the most famous footballers in the world, and the fans are screaming for a skinny kid from Bermuda! What a feeling! I wanted to get on straight away, but I wasn't ready for more than ten or fifteen minutes – but when the fans called my name ahead of all those top names on the bench, and one in particular . . . I'll keep the memory of that day with me for the rest of my life.

Sadly by this time George had made up his mind to leave. On the Monday after a defeat at Newcastle a week earlier I had come in for training to hear from the lads that Joe Royle had had a go at George and Paulo after the game. I do not know the exact reasons or what was said, but two days later George was gone.

George was very softly spoken and I have no doubt he must have felt embarrassed by the whole affair, and probably called his agent to explain he was not happy and told him to sort it out. I was training a few days later and stayed out to do extra work on finishing and other bits of my game. I had been out about half an hour and as I came in George was leaving. He said, 'Shaun, I'm leaving. Keep the good work up and all the best.' I told him I was sad to see him leave – how could I not be? – and I was a little surprised he had decided to resolve the situation so quickly; but I suppose when you're George Weah you would always have a queue of clubs waiting in line. I asked whether he had any boots or something to keep as a memento. I knew he had about ten pairs, but he said he didn't have anything left – the lads had cleared his locker out! Of all the days I decided to do extra training, I thought, it had to be that day. 'What about your training top?' I asked, but that had gone too. I asked him what his plans were and wished him well. He was a decent man with no airs or graces about him, and for all the tags he arrived with he was just a normal guy who was happy to pass on advice to the youngsters and blend in as best he could – that made me like him a lot. I think his coming to City opened the door for many more big names in the future because players will have looked at him and thought, 'If it's good enough for George . . .', and in that respect he was very good for the club. I just wanted to achieve a quarter of what he had.

There is just one story I will recount about George, and no doubt Nicky Weaver will remember it well. I was doing rehab on my knee and we had all gone for a relaxing day at David Lloyd's gym in Cheadle. I had been doing weights and timed things to finish so that I could join the rest of the lads in the pool. We were in the water and Nicky and I were talking to George about his culture and various other things, and as we talked Nicky decided to talk me up in front of George. He said jokingly, 'Well, George, I bet you haven't got a day named after you.' I nudged Nicky and stuck out my chest as if to say 'Keep it going!' but George paused for a moment and replied, 'No, I haven't got a day named after me'. Then, as I was thinking it was 1–0 to Goater, he said, 'But there's a 12-foot statue of me in the city centre back home'. I put my head under the water and swam to the other end of the pool! From the other end of the pool I looked back at Nicky who was smiling as if to say I'd got what I had deserved – I was just so pleased I hadn't mentioned it myself.

Back home, Anita was due any day. We had been trying for kids for a while but nothing was happening so we had tests which showed there was nothing wrong. We decided to try IVF to help things along, thinking that if it didn't work we would carry on trying as normal. We went through the procedure and after about four weeks they had told us everything looked good – doubly good, in fact, because we were expecting twin girls. I couldn't believe it. I was buzzing off it for weeks, and began buying parenting books and researching as much as I could so that I would be ready when our daughters arrived. Apart from the win at Blackburn that gave us both a fright, the pregnancy went well and on 3 October 2000 Amaya and Anais Goater entered the world.

I thought I was so far ahead of the game before the girls' arrival – I had Anita's hospital bag ready about three months into the pregnancy and it had been gathering dust since April. I had been practising the late-night dash for the hospital, getting Anita to test me on how long it would take to get ready and on our way when the big moment came, and got it down to about a minute. 'Go on, test me,' I would say, and she would sigh and say, 'All right, get ready for the hospital, Shaun'. 'Okay, give me a second', I replied. 'I've got the bag, I've got my wallet, I've got the keys . . .', and after going through a list of about ten things I would say, 'Okay, you straight? We're ready.' Of course, when the big moment did actually come, it was in the middle of the night and reality proved completely different from the staged drills I had insisted on. Anita nudged me to tell me she thought her waters had broken. 'Yeah, yeah, yeah,' I said, turning over to get back to my nice dream. She nudged me harder. 'Shaun, my waters just broke!' I was so knackered, I said, 'How'd you know? You've never been pregnant before'. So much for Mr Prepared . . .

Eventually I got up. 'Okay, what do you want me to do?' All the planning had gone out of the window and I was ambling around, definitely on Bermuda time. Anita checked in the bathroom to confirm her suspicions and by now I was finally waking up, but all I kept saying was 'Okay, okay, okay'. Anita had had enough. 'Right – get the bag, get the wallet and get your keys, get dressed and let's go!' We were soon in the car and on the way, but I was still a bit spaced out, smiling at the thought that my girls were finally on their way but driving along at a leisurely pace. Anita shouted, 'Shaun! Will you get a move on and stop going over bumps.' I said, 'Maybe I should stop and get some cash', and let's just say that Anita said she would rather not stop! Previous practice runs to the hospital had taken about twelve minutes, but I somehow managed to take twenty minutes for the real thing – and this at two in the morning. We settled in at Wythenshawe Hospital and waited around for things to start happening. We waited about five hours before I went and asked if anything was going to happen, and eventually it did and my beautiful girls arrived, six weeks early, by caesarian section. Amaya arrived first, weighing 5lb

6oz, and Anais weighed in at 5lb just a couple of minutes later. They had to be fed by tube because they didn't have the sucking reflex yet, but after a couple of days we returned home, happy to leave the hospital behind us. Within an hour or so of having the girls at home I knew that our house would never be tidy again! I was immensely proud, and was determined to give them everything I hadn't had, and we were just about as happy as could be. Joe gave me four days off, but of course that was never going to be enough. At least my job meant I would be home by early afternoon.

I recall the *Manchester Evening News* asking to take a picture of Anita, me and the girls and, although it was not really our scene, we agreed. A few days later I was in a newsagent's and saw a photo on the front page of a couple with twin babies and thought 'They look familiar – hell, that's us!' I had imagined it would be a little insert in the paper, but it was there on page 1, announcing 'The Goat Has Twins' – we had not expected that at all.

Back at the club I received a bag full of post with good wishes from the supporters; the lads were all congratulating me and giving me designer gifts for the girls. Next or Mothercare would have been fine, but it was the norm to buy expensive clothes for each others' kids. We gave some of the stuff away to charity, but it was really thoughtful of everyone; we really felt a strong bond with the club by this point, professionally and socially.

Soon it was time to concentrate on playing again, and with George Weah gone I reclaimed the No. 10 shirt I had worn on and off throughout my career. On the pitch things were not going to plan at all and the 5–0 defeat to Arsenal was particularly painful, especially as it was my full Premiership debut. I also missed a sitter in that game and was so gutted I forgot at the end to swap my shirt with any one of a dozen top stars – not the happy day I had imagined for my first ninety minutes in the top division. I was back playing again and was still waiting for my first goal, but at least I finally got to play against United, coming on as a sub. I was eager to pit my wits against Jaap Stam, who was – for me – the best defender in the world at the time. We were 1–0 down to David Beckham's free kick and chasing the game, and I came close to scoring when I had a tussle with Wes Brown and just missed beating Fabien Barthez to the ball. If I had reached it I would surely have equalised, but I only came on with ten minutes to go and ultimately it was not enough. I didn't see Fergie afterwards because he had gone to his son's wedding. The lads were really fired up by that because they felt he was being disrespectful – it was as if playing City was not that important.

Richard Dunne and Laurent Charvet had by now joined the club and it was clear that the money was sloshing around, too. I think Charvet was on a fair whack, and around this time you began to see flash cars in the car park – Porsches, Range Rovers, BMWs. Before that we had had 'we're doing okay' type of cars, but these were shouting out money. I liked Dunne – or Zidunne, as I christened him – and he settled in quickly. He was a big guy and deceptively quick – and young, too. I thought he was about 26 because he seemed to have been around for a while, but he was only 21 or so and I thought he had a lot of time ahead of him – and at a cost of £3.5m he has given the club fantastic service and been great value for money. He got his head down and worked hard, and came out with the lads whenever we went out. Throughout my career I found the best way of getting to know the lads was to go out with them when a new club opened or there was some function or other. It was a good way of settling in and fast-forwarded your relationship with the lads. I would always enjoy myself and the guys would respect the fact that I didn't drink. You have a laugh, tell a few stories and they think, 'Yeah, he's one of us' and you're in – it's a kind of initiation. Dunnie clicked with Bishop, Dicky and Steve Howey; and they were all good mates away from the club. It's great to see Dunnie has been made skipper now too. We were over in Ireland once after Tommy Wright had organised a trip and the majority of the lads would say the day after a heavy session, 'Shaun, don't come near me because I don't want to know what I was doing', but I would just say, 'Don't worry, you were good – you were all good'. I think they had their doubts!

We had some patchy form in the league and it was not until Everton came to Maine Road that we turned on the style and, finally, I scored my first Premiership goal. I remember it clearly. I was played in by a diagonal through ball; Weir was level with me but I shoulder-charged him enough to open myself up and I hit a cleanish strike. The ball went past the keeper and nestled in the corner. I celebrated in front of the Kippax and saluted my family in the box at the top of the stand. It was an important milestone in my career, and I hoped it would be the first of many.

Free of injury, I enjoyed a decent run in the team and just before Christmas Joe signed Darren Huckerby to give the rest of the strikers a kick up the backside. My agent Mark, a die-hard Coventry City fan, gave me the low-down on Darren, saying, 'Shaun, he will frustrate you but he is the kind of player who will attract a lot of players to him because of his runs – but you'll have to get on to him early about his passing'. There is an old saying that people will do to you what you allow them to, and although it has never been my style to go up to teammates and have a go, having been forewarned, I decided to let things go for three matches and see how it went. In those games Darren would often beat three or four players and then shoot from an acute angle. I knew exactly what Mark had meant and I had to deal with it straight away.

It meant that I had to make a gesture if he didn't pass to me when I thought he should have done, so that he knew I was upset with him. That is not something I like to do. Some players do it for the crowd, to say, 'See, crowd, I was free and he should have found me'. I wasn't into belittling teammates and getting the crowd on their back. But I could see signs that Darren was not always making the right choice. The next match we played together he beat a couple of players and then fired it wide. I held out my arms and said 'Darren, I was free!' and I have no doubt everyone was thinking, 'Didn't he even see Shaun?' It was for the good of us both, and fortunately he listened to what I was saying. Eventually we forged a great partnership, but it took time. He was an exciting player with plenty of pace and I enjoyed playing alongside him – once I got used to how he played and he understood my game. We were the only partnership to reach over 50 goals that season.

We missed Andy Morrison's presence that season; he was out with a knee injury for many months. He returned just after Christmas for a few games but it was tough for him and we missed his leadership. At that time there wasn't the pace around in the Premiership that there is today and Andy could have held his own, but he never seemed to get over his injury. This was a real shame because he could transmit confidence to the rest of the team, and with his motivational skills things might have turned out differently.

We beat Birmingham 3–0 in the FA Cup and I took up penalty-taking duties once again for this match. I am a great believer that, come the moment, the person on the pitch who is most confident should be the one to step up. Sometimes you can sense that the designated penalty taker is not in the right frame of mind so that's when you grab the ball and take it yourself, because it's all about belief at the time and there is no doubt among the lads who is going to take it. The last time I had taken one was in Division Two, and although it was a fantastic penalty I was just unlucky to face an exceptional goalkeeper that day. Fortunately I stuck this one away – I was confident enough and nobody else seemed up for it, so I thought, 'Why not?'

The Birmingham game was also Ian Bishop's last for the club. I liked Ian a lot and thought he was a very good player, and this is one area in which I did not agree with Joe Royle. I thought he should have played Ian a lot more. Our style was to battle with every team, something we had been used to from our days in the Second Division and we never really altered our mindset. I can understand reluctance to change a successful formula. Jeff and Jim Whitley were far better than anything else around that Second Division, and also the First Division. Moving up to the Premiership we needed more ball-players, but Joe stuck with the battlers like Jeff Whitley and Alfie Haaland and we were not creating enough opportunities. I would look at the team and wonder where my goals were going to come from – who could play the killer balls or the right weighted ball into space for me to run on to? Kevin Horlock could do it, and he was the person I would look to for a supply line, but he was out for the season with injury and I didn't get many assists from Mark Kennedy. At my previous teams I would think, 'I'll get so many chances through so-and-so, he's a good crosser and then there are the knock-downs and scraps around the box', but in this team I could not see from where those chances would come.

Huckerby and Wanchope could create a few of their own chances out of nothing, but as a forward you still need good service to operate at optimum levels. Joe would say after a defeat that we had been unlucky and we had battled hard, and that same line continued throughout the season. I thought to myself, 'We can't be unlucky thirty-eight times in one season'. We needed to utilise the creative players more, and Ian Bishop was pretty much our only inventive midfielder; he used to get us playing and that would result in a better supply to the front players.

I wished Ian all the best as he headed off for Miami Fusion, and because I always had an eye on America I told him I'd be in touch. Ian's a really great guy, the sort who would say, 'You can have my wallet, take my car keys, but don't touch my drink'. I would miss him around Maine Road and the team would miss him, because I think if he had played most games there would have been a different outcome at the end of the season.

I was back on the bench for the match with Derby and also started as sub when Coventry City came to Maine Road for an FA Cup fourth round tie. For this game my agent Mark would have split loyalties, and I think his ideal scenario was Coventry winning 3–2 with me scoring both our goals. As it was, I came on to score the only goal – a last-minute winner. Mark later said he was pleased for me but absolutely gutted overall. I celebrated by running over to the corner flag near the North Stand, where our fans usually were. I was shouting and gesturing to the fans and generally enjoying the moment – only they were not our fans! It was then I realised that the Coventry fans had been allocated an area usually reserved for home supporters, and I could see one or two guys jump up aggressively, shouting abuse at me as I reached the corner. Like Man City, Coventry's shirts are sky blue, and this may have added to my mistake. I carried on running until I reached the halfway line, safe in the knowledge these were our fans, but behind me crowd trouble had broken out, with the irate Coventry fans obviously thinking I had set out to incite them. But it was entirely innocent – I just hadn't realised.

Later that week Health and Safety officers came to the club and I had to watch a video of a game between Birmingham and Aston Villa where they explained what happened on match days, how things developed inside the ground and what it could lead to outside the ground. I suppose I got a bit of a ticking off, even though it had all been entirely good intention on my part. It opened my eyes to how our celebrations and reactions on the pitch can lead to crowd problems and how innocent people can get caught up in it all. It also made me realise how I could help more as a player. From then on I made a point of ensuring that I knew where our fans were, and where the opposition fans were sitting.

That goal against Coventry seemed to have made up Joe's mind that I would be starting the majority of games from then on until the end of the season. Andrei Kanchelskis was signed on loan from Rangers. I thought he was a good signing. He was a fast, direct player with a terrific reputation from his days at United and Everton and I thought he could only help our cause. Our form in the league was not great, so the FA Cup was a welcome distraction and the team we drew in the last sixteen would give me the opportunity to realise a boyhood dream – Liverpool, at Anfield.

Having been a Liverpool fan as a kid, it was an amazing feeling to run out onto the field of my dreams. I thought back to the days when I would watch John Barnes and imagine myself scoring goals at Anfield. I fulfilled my dream by scoring in the first half – an incredible feeling, even though a slight deflection took it past the keeper. It wasn't at the Kop End, but I was happy to take it. We lost 4–2 that day, but the week after I was able to cross another dream off my list.

We travelled to Newcastle for a crucial Premiership game, and I remember seeing our fans way up in the clouds in the corner of St James' Park as I warmed up. This was Alan Shearer's stomping ground. What better place to leave another mark than at the home of one of the greatest strikers in English football? If I scored, I would treat the Newcastle fans to a Shearer-type celebration, running off to the corner with one arm raised. When I did actually score, my mind went totally blank and I ran towards our fans with no thought of Alan Shearer – what a chance missed. I was proud to have scored the winner in the backyard of another of my mentors. Steve Howey had a bruising encounter with Shearer that day, and when the game was over they walked up to each other, bloodied and bruised, and shook hands. I thought that was brilliant. I walked over and asked Steve whether he would ask Shearer for his shirt and he gave it to me; that's something I will keep proudly in my collection.

I found the net in two of the next three games and was not concerned by the loan arrival of Egil Ostenstadt from Blackburn. I had seen him play over the years, and I knew if I just kept doing what I was doing I would be fine. The next match was at home to Arsenal. They just tore us apart, and some of the football they played was sublime. We were 4–0 down inside twenty minutes and I knew we were playing the champions. Thierry Henry was so fast that he passed Richard Dunne as though he was standing still – and Dunney was pretty fast when he got going. I received a ball just inside their half. Freddie Ljungberg was pressuring me from behind so I controlled it with my right foot, then with my second touch using the inside of my left foot, did a Cruyff-like turn, which took me in the direction that he had just come from, and got a 'Whoooooo!' from the crowd. Arsenal were awesome that day.

We then went to Leicester, where we won 2–1. Paulo scored an audacious back-heel, but that was Paulo. I distinctly remember my goal because Tim Flowers was in goal and there was a cross played over the top between him and me, a ball neither of us really wanted to go for, but we had to. As we went up for the ball I turned my head away; Tim had his eyes shut and the ball hit me on the back of the head and went into the net. I landed with my back to goal and we were both wondering where the ball was when all my teammates ran over to me to celebrate. I didn't mind how they went in – I would take any goal that came my way. A year later, when Tim arrived at City on loan, he walked into the dressing room and I said, 'Here comes another one of my victims!' Tim laughed, saying, 'You can't be claiming that goal'. 'Take a look at my repertoire,' I replied, 'that was a good one.' He was another former England keeper against whom I had managed to find the net, but I still had a few names to cross off my list.

One of my biggest disappointments of the season was in the next game, when we played United at Old Trafford. I was desperate to go back there and prove a point, so to find out I was on the bench was a huge let-down. I felt I was in great form and could not believe Joe had dropped me, and he probably still won't know until he reads this. I was really annoyed, and Gerard Wiekens said, 'Look Shaun, I know you're frustrated and yes, you should be playing, but you've got to think of the team'. Five minutes later I managed to put my disappointment aside and returned to the dressing room, saying, 'Come on lads, big game today – let's get into them'. I was totally behind the team, but when the game kicked off and there was banter between the fans it began to hit me again, and I thought, 'I'm supposed to be out there'. Then as the clock started ticking down we were losing 1–0, and I warmed up a few times thinking, 'Okay, I'll get twenty-five minutes', then, 'Maybe twenty minutes', but as it reached the last fifteen and I started warming up once more I was becoming more and more frustrated. I warmed up yet again, trying to show Joe that I was ready. Eventually I came on with five minutes left, and was so mad that I didn't care who I was playing against – I just wanted the ball, and if it came to me, I didn't care about the team, I was going to do what I wanted to do, completely opposite to my usual attitude of 'team first'. I don't think I had time to do anything, but at least we drew 1–1. This was also the game in which Roy Keane scythed down Alfie Haaland. I was on the bench at the time and my initial thought was that it was a terrible tackle. Watching it on video later, I could see Roy had really gone in to do him. Keane leant over Alfie after the tackle and said something along the lines of 'That's for the tackle you did on me at Leeds'.

If I was ever on the end of a bad tackle, I always gave the player the benefit of the doubt, although when Andy Morrison and Dicky were on the pitch they were likely to take out their own form of retribution on my behalf.

With three games to go we knew we had to win them all to be in with a chance of staying up. The first of the trio was at home to West Ham. I scored the only goal and was chuffed to have put one past England keeper David James – that was another off my wish-list. After the game I found they had credited it as an Ian Pearce own goal – that was my goal, trust me, and I am reclaiming it to make it Goater 4, England 0. With the teams around us winning, the trip to Ipswich became even more important. We started well and when I had a chance I stole in to put us ahead, but injured my knee and as a result had to go off. We lost 2–1, and that confirmed our relegation. I was sick that we had gone down after just one year at the top; the only consolation was ending the season as top scorer with eleven goals from twenty-five starts – twelve if the goal against West Ham had stood – and this despite missing part of the season because of my knee injury. I was proud to continue my ratio of a goal every two games in the Premiership, and despite the likes of Weah, Wanchope, Huckerby and Kanchelskis playing up front that season, I was the one who topped the scoring charts. That felt good.

CHAPTER TWELVE

Wolves at the Door

I was shopping at Marks & Spencer's with Anita when my mobile rang. It was Gerard Wiekens and his first words were, 'Have you heard the news?' I said I had not heard anything that day as I had been out and about. 'Joe Royle's been sacked', he said. 'Yeah, yeah, you're just having me on', I replied, because we had been known to wind each other up. But Gerard was insistent. 'Honestly, it's just been on the news – Joe Royle has been sacked.' One or two City fans came up to say hello, but they said nothing about it. As soon as I got home I switched on Sky Sports, and it was still a breaking news story. Joe had won us successive promotions and although we had been relegated I didn't think he deserved to be sacked. It completely threw me. I phoned Gerard and said, 'He should have played me against United!' It was only a joke, and we both spoke of feeling for Joe. My first thought was to call and wish him all the best, but thinking it over, I reckoned either his phone would be turned off or he would be constantly

WOLVES AT THE DOOR

busy. I knew I would have a chance to speak to him at some point, but in the meantime I called his secretary, Julia McCrindle, knowing he'd still have some loose ends to tie up at the club, to pass on my regards and best wishes for the future.

Joe had brought me to City, stuck with me at times when it would have been far easier to drop me, and given me the platform to go and express myself. I honestly believed he would have taken us straight back up, because if Joe knew anything it was how to get a team promoted from Division One – we had come back up and there would be loads more goals along the way. The question was, who would be taking over and when? The lads were all trying to guess who might come in, and although everyone on the outside thinks we are clued up with inside knowledge, the truth is that we know just about the same as the bloke down the pub – we hadn't a clue. A few names were mentioned, but I did not find out who the new man was until I had returned home to Bermuda.

Back in Bermuda I generally switch off from football and take no interest in it whatsoever. People might want to say, 'Hey, great season', or 'Unlucky' for the first week or so, but that's about as far as it goes. Then someone asked me, 'Do you know who your new manager is?' When I said I didn't, he told me it was Kevin Keegan. 'What? For real?' I said, and I was buzzing about it for days. He was a legendary striker for England, a former England manager too, and I thought he would teach me all I needed to know and give me all the ingredients I wanted to add to my game and take me to the next level.

I knew he had seen me in action because of the hat-trick I'd scored against his Fulham side a couple of years earlier, so I looked forward to returning for pre-season and getting started again.

The first day back is all about weighing-in, exchanging pleasantries and catching up with the lads – you only spend about an hour actually training. Our first meeting with Keegan was as a team, and he said the usual things new managers always seem to say, about being glad to be there, a great future ahead, and all that had happened in the past was all in the past and everyone was starting with a clean slate and on the same level. I was one of probably four players who still had not met Keegan personally. A few lads had come in early for extras and some would have returned a day or so before scheduled because of injury. I just shook his hand and said, 'All right, gaffer'. Keegan made some great early signings in Stuart Pearce and Eyal Berkovic, and a new fitness coach had arrived, too, a Colombian called Juan Carlos Osorio.

To this day Osorio remains the best coach I've ever had. When I first met him I said, 'So you're gonna have us running around trees just like all the other coaches', and he replied, 'No, I'm a bit different from that – I've played myself so I know players don't want to run around fields all day. My training is football specific. As a footballer you don't ever sprint further than four to five seconds and my training is based around that.' He promised there would be no long runs or anything like that, and he was as good as his word and was a terrific fitness coach. I remember playing a pre-season game at Huddersfield. 'Juan,' I said, 'I don't feel fit', and he said, 'Shaun, you've done enough, you'll be all right in the game'. As it was, I felt sharp and alert and he hadn't had us on one long run. It was amazing, because I came from the old school of training. I was used to exhausting runs that ended up with me being sick, so Juan was a breath of fresh air – unique in his style and totally original. He was one of the first of his kind. Juan is Number One in my book – and he knows he's good, too.

As for Eyal Berkovic, everyone knew about his training ground spat with John Hartson but I like to get to know people properly before making any judgements. Eyal had a different way about him. He would appear abrupt sometimes, but when you got to know him properly you realised it was just the way he was and that he did not intend it in a bad way. If you could see through his ways that was when you got to know Eyal, and he was a good guy and an excellent footballer. Players like Eyal raised the bar and he was a great talent. At keep-ball sessions there was no way you could get it off him. Everyone hated to play against him because he would come towards you, give a little shuffle, sidestep you and be away. He was a great team player and never passed to anyone more than 20 yards away. He always played you balls that were easy to control and accurately played to your feet along the ground. I do not think he ever used his instep except to shoot. He would bring everyone into the game and make sure everybody had a touch. Even when you were struggling he would give you an easy pass and provide an easy option to pass back, so you could build up your confidence. He could make us play! The best I had seen up till then was Ian Bishop, but Eyal was perhaps three levels higher. He fitted perfectly into Keegan's blueprint, which was, basically, 'You're not in my team if you don't want the ball'. He wanted his defenders to be available for the ball when it was in the keeper's arms and he just wanted us to play, play, play.

I was ready and raring to go for the new season when I heard a whisper that initially deflated me and then gave me all the motivation I needed to go out and show Keegan what I could do. Apparently, he had tried to sell me to David Jones's Wolves for £1.2m during the close season and it was quite a near thing. Before the new season started I had a call from Wolves chief executive Jez Moxey, sounding me out about a move. I was absolutely gutted that Keegan was willing to sell me without giving me a chance. It got to the point that I was resigned to leaving and told Moxey that if City did not want me I would rather go to a club that did, even though the words were sticking in my throat. The deal never materialised and I heard later that it was because a director told Keegan, 'You can't sell Shaun – he's been our top scorer for the last three seasons'. So far as I was concerned, I wanted to show Keegan what I was about.

I think he was hoping that I would not produce and that then, maybe a dozen games into the season, he could move me on. I was sick because I wanted to learn so much from him and I knew he didn't want me around – and there's no worse feeling to have in football. Anita, level-headed as ever, told me I just had to get the whole thing out of my head and prove him wrong. It was about a month before I managed to do that, but until I did so I still wanted Wolves to come in and resurrect the deal. To want me out of the way so early in his time at the club made me deeply suspicious of Keegan, and that did not change until the day I left Maine Road.

Surprisingly, then, I was named in his first starting line-up as we took on Watford on a Saturday evening televised game. Eyal was superb and I scored our first of the night, heading home a Charvet cross, and we went on to win 3–0. We played a brand of football that was typical Keegan and we sent out a message to the rest of the division that night. Playing with someone like Stuart Pearce was really good, too. He had been there, seen it and got the T-shirt, and his winning mentality was infectious. On the Friday before a game, if there was a ball to be won in training he would slide in and make sure he won it. That was Stuart.

Regardless of what Keegan thought, I made my best ever start to a season, grabbing a couple against Crewe in our third match and a hat-trick away at (ker-ching!) Burnley – who were top, before the game – to make it six in four games. I was playing with better players and was getting great service, too – and I had a burning motivation to prove the manager wrong. I knew that if I kept scoring I would make it difficult for him to drop me.

Our 4–0 defeat at West Bromwich then allowed us to see a different side of Keegan. He went ballistic afterwards, and also did something none of the lads particularly liked. In the after-match interviews he said things like, 'They were rubbish', or, 'That was no team of mine', anything to disassociate himself from us, whereas if we won it was 'we' or 'my'. I didn't like that at all.

I could put bad performances or defeats out of my system quickly by turning up to training with a positive attitude, determined to start afresh. The funny thing was, Keegan was exactly the same. He would crack jokes with us all and we would think, 'Wait a minute, you were ripping into us a few days ago and now you want to be our best mate?' I was naturally positive and in high spirits because my goals return was still good, but there was already a bit of resentment building among the lads. I scored in our midweek League Cup game at Notts County, and before the league match with Birmingham, Ali Benarbia joined the club.

When any new player arrived at the club I always wanted to impress in the first session he took part in, so he would have a positive image of me. Don't get me wrong, I wanted to do well in every session, it was just something within me I needed to do. We had a bit of a loosener session and a five-a-side game as well as walking through a few set-pieces, and during this time I observed Ali at close quarters. My initial impression was that he did not seem any different from what we already had. Obviously you cannot judge someone in such a brief span of time, but everything Ali did that day was safe, whereas I was looking for a little turn or something special in his game. Walking away from training that day I felt that I hadn't seen anything that suggested this guy was a quality player. That was until he actually made his debut.

When I saw Ali get the ball I made a run, but stopped only to see the ball placed perfectly, a split-second later, in the direction I had been running. It happened a few times during the game, and each pass was wasted because I thought the ball would never get to me, but each time Ali delivered perfectly weighted passes. It happened a couple of times in our next game, and then it clicked – I had to keep running when this guy had the ball because he would find you. It was like a hallelujah moment – at last! I spoke to Kyle Lightbourne shortly after Ali's arrival and I told him the only person I could think of with a talent like his was Diego Maradona – that might seem over the top, but he was right up there as far as I was concerned. Ali could always find you with a pass, and for a striker it was a dream come true. I felt as if I had won the lottery.

We lost at Coventry 4–3 in the next game (the one time my agent got the better of me) and then it was away to Sheffield Wednesday, where the team – and Ali in particular – were on fire. We beat them 6–2 and Ali played a ball to me through about four players and just behind the last defender, Danny Maddix. It was so accurate that Maddix stopped his run, thinking the keeper would get it first, but I was learning quickly and sure enough it carried through to me and I took it past the keeper and tapped it home. It was impossible to defend against and the mark of genius – a perfect pass from an unbelievable talent. The fact I scored six goals in Ali's four games proved he had been fantastic for me, but I also realised that he needed me, too. For Ali to be at his devastating best he needed the killer run and that was my forte – he was my satnav! It might have been early in the season, but if you had asked Sheffield Wednesday that day they would have said we were awesome – and they had just been beaten by the champions.

A goal against Walsall – you might call it a typical Goater goal – following up a shot by Paulo and tucking the ball home when it came back off the post, took my tally to twelve in ten games. A week later and we were hammered 4–0 at home to Wimbledon.

Michael Hughes had a great game that day, but we did not perform at all. They had guys on Ali to stop us playing but we didn't have an answer on the day – no Plan B. It was something of a freak result, and one we put right four days later when we beat Birmingham 6–0 in the League Cup. Stockport was always a tough game for us, and we went 2–0 down to a Tony Dinning goal; his celebration hurt because he did what Nicky Weaver had done at Wembley, running 5 yards from the goal and then beckoning to Nick to catch him. It was quite a clever celebration but it got our backs up, mine in particular, and I thought there was no way he was leaving Maine Road still smiling, having taken the rip like that. We fought back to draw 2–2.

Things were going well, but a 2–1 defeat at Preston was a blow, especially when the header I challenged for was cleared to the halfway line to Jon Macken, who hit a long looping volley over Nick's head and into the net from about 50 yards out. It was a fantastic goal, and no more than they deserved. Afterwards Keegan berated me for not winning the header; when the chips were down there was a definite pattern forming of 'I'll have a go at Shaun'. Whenever something went wrong or we played badly, he singled me out. He rarely said anything to Paulo or Hucks, and I came to expect it.

Arthur Cox would also speak in the dressing room, and he was a man I listened to. I began to switch off to Keegan's rants because they did not really say anything, whereas Arthur spoke constructively and you could always learn from him. I recall one game where I scored a goal in the first half and was on the top of my game; I didn't want the half to end. I gave the ball away once, but was leading the line well and went into the dressing room buzzing and fully expecting Keegan to say, 'Give the ball to Shaun, he's got the beating of these guys', but that was the last thing he had in his mind. He went around the lads saying, 'Well done, you played well there', or, 'Unlucky, keep at it'. Then he got to me and he started having a go at me for losing the ball on one occasion. I had been tearing the defence apart and thought, 'That's all you remember?' I answered him back, 'Gaffer, I only lost the ball on one occasion – tell me the other times I lost it?' I had come in buzzing and he completely deflated me. He only seemed to recall the last thing the players had done, or something significant they had done in the half. To me, his man-management was poor, but without my realising it, he was giving me all the motivation I needed because I wanted to shove his words back down his throat. In all the time I worked under him he never looked me in the eye and said, 'You played really well today, Shaun' – I don't think he could have, in all honesty. Our relationship was strained, to say the least, but I was determined to have the last laugh. I think the fans were almost dictating that I played, and he must have resented that – but I kept scoring.

A goal against Grimsby and another at Nottingham Forest – which was my easiest goal ever, as anyone who saw it will confirm. The keeper rolled the ball out for the defender, then ran back, but the defender was running away and in the confusion all I had to do was run up, take it round him and slot it home. A goal at Barnsley, and then the fourth hat-trick of my City career in a 4–1 win over Gillingham kept my run going. Eyal Berkovic had returned from injury, so with him and Ali in the team I was in striker heaven. With these two players in the side I knew that every match we played I would get at least one good scoring chance because they would always create something, and for a forward there really is no better feeling. All I had to do was work out what I would do when the chance presented itself – header, volley, chip, shin or backside – whatever! On a good day they would make four chances for me, but we had a midfield to die for and I was hungry! Feed the Goat – and they did!

CHAPTER THIRTEEN

Record Breakers

T he worst thing chairman David Bernstein could have said to me was that he would buy me a flash car if I could hit the thirty-goal mark before Christmas 2001 – that put me right off, and despite having eighteen goals in eighteen games, I kind of dried up for a few games. I took his word literally, but every time I had an opportunity a vision of a Porsche flashed across my mind and I fluffed it.

We were still riding high at the top of Division One and Keegan brought in Christian Negouai to bolster the midfield, claiming he was one of the most exciting signings he had ever made. I was not sure about that, but I know Negouai came close to ending Hucks' season with an awful tackle in training. We had been doing some one-on-ones and with Negouai being a defensive midfielder, Darren took him on. The tackle on him left a gaping gash on his shin and that moment pretty much summed up Negouai's time at City. He got off to a bad start and never really had the luck he needed to make it. He was neat and tidy and could do a job, but he had a habit of shooting himself in the foot, and the few first-team appearances he did make usually ended in some kind of controversy. He seemed to be always either injured or suspended, and much of it seemed to be self-inflicted.

In the league we travelled to Millwall with the unusual sight of an empty away end, the two clubs having agreed to ban away support for this fixture. I had become used to the way Millwall fans behaved, but that night Shaun Wright-Phillips and I received the kind of racial abuse that was sickening even for them. It was not nearly as scary as it had been in the past, and I warmed up with a smile on my face, even though one thug in particular was, forgive the pun, trying to get my goat – but failing, of course. The Millwall fans shouted abuse, despite there being one or two black faces among the home support. It was a bizarre situation; and I wondered how these people could attend the games there when the racism was so rife. I still felt that the club should be shut down, but as that was unlikely to ever happen, my only answer was to score against them. Huckerby's celebration was inspired – he ran to the empty stands and applauded, his hands above his head, and Shaun and I joined him doing the same thing and loved it. Better still, Wrighty later scored a cracker – his first goal for the club – to complete a 3–2 win, and a very enjoyable night's work. I moved on to twenty-three goals as we continued through January. When we beat leaders Burnley 5–1 I was not among the scorers. I could not understand why my direct debit account against them had failed for the first time I could remember. We kept on winning, and our 4–1 victory at Ipswich – now a Premiership club – in the FA Cup boosted our confidence to new levels. We were flying towards automatic promotion.

Having the likes of Ali and Eyal in the team at the same time created a dilemma for Keegan, but I was firmly behind his theory that playing them both was the best option, because we dominated games when they played together. If you had asked the full-backs, they would probably have said just one flair player would be enough, because once our attacks broke down the opposition would be straight at our back four – there was no protection from them in the middle. Eyal and Ali playing allowed someone like Danny Tiatto to play a game more suited to his style, which was out wide and being able to get stuck in and play aggressively – he didn't need to worry about creating chances.

Niclas Jensen was another new signing, and a very cultured defender. He made his debut at Ipswich and impressed me immediately in the game at Portman Road. This guy was a player, and I do not think he gave the ball away in the whole match. He played great passes up to me and had an understanding of how strikers like to receive the ball. In my opinion some of the most important players in the game are full-backs, because the minute the keeper catches the ball the team pushes up and the full-backs go wide and, more often than not, the ball goes out to them. Straight away they are looking for the strikers – and Jensen knew how to play perfectly weighted passes into our feet.

Stuart Pearce was a great defender and a born leader, but some of his passes to me were like shots! I used to tell him before games, 'Stuart, you're hitting the ball into me too hard, I can't control it'. I guess his theory was if it didn't get cut out, it was not his problem any more. I wondered whether my touch was not as good as other players' in England. Did he change his game when he fired them in for Shearer and Owen? Surely not; he must have played the same way. Sometimes I would leave one of his passes alone because I thought it must be intended for somebody behind me – it had that much pace on it. I had to ask for half-pace passes so I had a chance of controlling them, but Jensen's passes were ideal and he is one of the best left-backs I ever played with.

Most of Keegan's signings had been a success, with the exception of Negouai, but new faces meant more departures, and Dicky finally gave up his bid to win over Keegan and left for Leicester City. His ratio was not fantastic – about one goal in three or four games – but if anyone could get away with selling such a popular player, it was Keegan. Observing Dicky had taught me what was needed to impress the City fans, and when I had started adding attributes of his game to mine, things had turned around for me. His determination and energy would be missed, as well as his infectious personality, and I was sad to see him leave. Jon Macken was another new face at the club, signed for £5.5m from Preston, and I was concerned at his arrival because I knew what Keegan thought about me, and I knew I had to keep producing to keep him out of the team.

Jon had scored an incredible goal against us earlier in the season and, as he had been a Manchester United junior, I knew he was a decent player with good technique, but his goals-per-game ratio was not fantastic. It kept me on my toes and he made a great start, coming on to replace me at Bradford and scoring. I think that was the only time I felt jealous of a new player because he had been successful in his first game. It was worse because I had had a couple of easy chances and not scored, but I was not about to give up my place without a fight.

The team kept winning and the goals kept going in for me, and the home win over Sheffield Wednesday took me to twenty-nine for the season. Then I hit a wall. There was a lot of talk about my becoming the first person to hit thirty goals in a season since

Francis Lee in 1972 and I did not find the net for the next three games. To emulate a player like Lee was a major feat, and that played on my mind during a couple of games but finally, away to Crewe, I managed it.

Before kick-off Darren Huckerby came up to me and said, 'Don't worry, you're getting your goal today – I'm going to set you up'. I had been dragging balls wide and snatching at chances, and despite our being under pressure from Crewe, Ali scored an incredible goal to put us ahead. Then Darren got the ball out wide, beat a couple of defenders and drew another one in, and then slid the ball across to me to run on to. I hit it and watched as it went in, and the relief was incredible. I thought that I could relax again – the pressure was off. It was a milestone for me because it was my first thirty-goal haul; it had also been a long time since a City player had scored that many, and I was appreciative of Darren for helping me reach it. Our partnership would top fifty goals that season, and part of the success was that we had an understanding. I knew that Darren might shoot four times out of five if he got the chance, but I also knew that for the fifth opportunity he would slip me in. It was important that I encouraged that side of his game, because he needed to play his natural game to be at his best.

Two games later and I was headed for my first early bath for City. I had got a little caught up in the derby atmosphere as we took on Stockport at Edgeley Park. We had been under a bit of pressure and I was on the back post as a cross came over. Carlo Nash was caught off his line and as a looping header came in I reached up, thinking, 'I don't want this ball to go in', and hit the ball with my hand, then tumbled into the back of the net. I had not heard Stuart Pearce shouting right behind me. I was sent off for the first time in my career, but Stockport missed the penalty – not that it mattered because we lost 2–1.

Keegan laid into me as though I had cost us an FA Cup final, and said he would have preferred to be 1–0 down with eleven men, but it all happened in a split second and I still do not know why I stuck my hand up. I apologised to the lads, but Keegan said, 'Sorry is not good enough'. I switched off, because I knew his angle would be negative rather than constructive. If you are a player whom the manager likes he will forgive you in a situation like that, but I never got that from him.

Next up was a return to my old stomping ground as we travelled to Millmoor to take on Rotherham. I warned the lads about the sloping pitch and about the fans being right on top of you. It was the only club I had played for where a fan made his way to the tunnel to wait for me so that he could knock seven bells out of me! He had felt I was lazy and that I was not doing it, and as he was 20 stone and built like a brick outhouse I was not going to argue with him. He told me I was ripping off the club. 'At £400 a week, I ain't ripping you off, you're ripping me off!', I thought, and was glad the stewards were on hand to keep him back. But that's how their fans were; they grafted hard all day and expected their team to do the same, and if they didn't they would give you dog's abuse and you got the impression that they would take it further if they had the chance.

On arrival I looked around the dressing rooms and I could see nothing had changed since my departure. They might have moved up a couple of divisions, but the paintwork was still flecked and stained with age and everything else was as it had been. I got a mixed reception, but Rotherham is a working man's town and I took the odd jeer mingled with applause to be a sign of appreciation. They were not the sort of fans to welcome you back with open arms, but that did not mean they didn't respect you. We drew 1–1 and it was a hard afternoon, as it always seemed to be, but I was proud to return as part of such a huge club. It showed I had moved on, although I am acutely aware of the things I learned playing for Rotherham, and appreciative of the opportunities they gave me.

I played in our next game against Nottingham Forest but was put on the bench for the Wolves match, with Jon Macken preferred up front. I was disappointed because it was a big game for us, and I couldn't believe Keegan had dropped me with thirty goals in the bank – that took a bit of bottle. I knew my chance would come again, so I switched my focus to the team and Jon played well as we won 2–0. I then served a one-match ban against Barnsley, a game we won 5–1 to confirm us as champions. Keegan then said I could choose which of the final two games of the season I wanted to play in. I wanted to play in them both!

I played at Gillingham and was determined to end the season on a high. I also knew if I played well it would most likely guarantee my place for the final game of the season against Portsmouth, which would be a party atmosphere that I did not want to miss. We played some nice stuff, and Ali was running the show. He played the ball in to me and I played it back to him, just inside the box. He back-heeled it back but flipped it off the ground at the same time, so I struck a sweet volley low and hard past the Gillingham keeper for one of my favourite goals for City. I was well pleased with that, and I knew Keegan could not drop me now for the Portsmouth game.

We beat Pompey 3–1 and I got my thirty-second of the season, although I cannot recall much about it. I do remember watching Stuart Pearce stepping up to take a last-minute penalty in his last career game. He had scored a fantastic ninety-nine goals and this gave him the chance to end his distinguished career with his hundredth goal. I wondered how he would approach it and watched in horror – like everyone else – as he powered it past the post. I knew then why fans said 'typical City', because you could not write an ending like that. I reckon Dave Beasant would have let it in if it had been on target, but knowing how most keepers are perhaps not. Stuart took the miss well, but he must have felt devastated. We would miss his professionalism in the dressing room, because you cannot replace a player like that, even if he was 39 at the time.

I enjoyed the lap of honour after the match with my daughter Amaya (Anais was a little bit too shy to walk round Maine Road in front of 34,000 people and I could understand that). We all went on the stage with the trophy and it was a very proud moment because we had won it by playing attractive, stylish football. I looked over at Keegan and thought, 'This guy has motivated me all season and he doesn't even know it.'

I then picked up the Player of the Year award from the City fans. Things had really come full circle for me. I'd reached a point with the team and the fans where I wasn't scared to miss and could play without restraint. It was an honour and I also made it into the PFA Division One team of the season – another honour, this time from my fellow-pros, and one that meant, in essence, that they didn't like playing against me!

We may have been back in the Premiership too, where we deserved to be, but I was still suspicious of the manager's intentions and wondered what was in store for me during the coming season.

CHAPTER FOURTEEN
Who Let the Goat Out?

While I was home in Bermuda I heard that City had signed Nicolas Anelka, who I thought was an excellent acquisition for the club. He was a good player; I had seen him play in the Champions League final and knew of his exploits at Arsenal. He had a bit of a history of being problematic at his previous clubs, but I liked to take people as I found them and that was how I would base our friendship. By the time I had returned to England, Marc Vivien Foe, Sylvain Distin and Peter Schmeichel had all arrived, too – big names with lofty reputations – but my approach was that I had seen a few expensive strikers off in the past so why couldn't I see off a few more? I was up for the challenge, that was for sure. I did not come in thinking I was past my sell-by date, just that this was the level I had aimed for and now I had to get down to the hard work again. But I also had to contend with Keegan and his views as to what I could and could not do, and that was an entirely different battle.

I knew Anelka could benefit my game because he would attract defenders and create space for me, and he also had the ability to make chances out of nothing. I hoped we would get the chance to play alongside each other. Anelka illustrated that we were paying out a lot of big salaries now, but that did not bother me because I felt that if you were happy to sign for a sum one week, you shouldn't complain if somebody signed a week later and got more, because you were fine the week before. I just thought 'Well done' to those lads if that was what the club wanted to pay them.

There were a lot of strikers at Maine Road now, but so long as I felt I had a chance my future was with City and nobody would have been able to entice me away. Keegan was still my motivation, although he still did not know.

Training was going well, and I knew that if Keegan wanted to push me out of the picture he would have the City fans to deal with because they were 100 per cent behind me and would no doubt be keen to speak on my behalf. If he wanted his own big-name signings in he was going to be under pressure from the supporters, because they always seemed to want me to play and their backing was unwavering and unconditional. I hoped that things would go well and I could overcome the latest set of hurdles placed in front of me, but it was not until several games into the campaign that I finally played – as I had sustained a toe fracture in July 2002 in a friendly game against Huddersfield Town, when one of their young players landed on my foot – coming on as a substitute at Arsenal. Keegan preferred the Anelka/Huckerby pairing, and I knew I had to bide my time yet again and wait for a chance. I had been here before and knew what it took to ride the storm. Yet I was particularly hurt when Keegan started a home game against Blackburn with reserve team winger Chris Shuker up front instead of me. I asked Keegan why he had not given me the chance to start the game and he gave me the usual waffle. He was searching for a partner for Anelka, but it seemed he was determined to play anyone rather than me. However, I did come on as substitute and within a few minutes Danny Tiatto was sent off for a foul on David Thompson. We were losing 2–0 but Anelka pulled one back and I scored a late equaliser to secure a 2–2 draw. I think Keegan actually made some positive comments about me after the game – a first! He spoke of Tiatto's tackle to the press, but I do not recall him saying anything to him in the dressing room.

Another striker who had arrived for big money during the summer was Matias Vuoso. He never got a chance at City and he could never understand why Keegan never gave him one. I played a few reserve team games with him and he was not a bad player; he had good technique and was not bad in the air, but I recall Keegan saying to him on one occasion, 'If you don't learn English, you won't play in my team'. I wondered how he could say that to a player he had bought from Argentina. Hadn't he scouted him properly? Or was this an excuse not to play him? He should have known this would be a problem, yet he had paid £4m for him at a time when Argentina's economy was rock bottom. I went out with him and a few of the lads once, and Matias said, 'Why Keegan no play you?' His English was much better when he was drunk! 'Keegan no like you?' he continued. I told him that was for Keegan to answer.

Around this time I had an unforgettable experience over a period of about 16 hours. A few months earlier I'd been asked to carry the Commonwealth Games Jubilee baton from Maine Road to the City of Manchester Stadium on 25 July 2002, and on the day I had to be up at 6.30am to complete the task, running with City Ladies captain Jane Clark. In fact, I'm reliably informed I was the first-ever City player to enter the new stadium, which is another honour. Later that day, David

Beckham handed the baton to the Queen to open the Games and I was again privileged to be asked by the Bermudian team to walk alongside the flag-bearer at the opening ceremony. I'd been asked to be Bermuda's Team Attaché a few months back and this was my reward, though the toe injury I'd sustained meant I had to hobble around the running track somewhat. It was an incredible occasion and seeing City's future home packed in all its glory (though there was still one tier buried beneath tons of soil) was an amazing sight.

Returning to the football, Eyal Berkovic's midfield partner, Ali, did not have the impact I had imagined he would have in the Premiership. I could not wait to see him take on the likes of Patrick Vieira and Roy Keane, because I thought he would wipe the floor with them. But I also noticed Ali was coming out of the gaffer's office a lot more regularly. I thought that the more he came out of that office the less respect he would have with the lads, and up to that point it was total – what he said went.

He also started taking over a few training sessions with the forwards, concentrating on movement. Coupled with his frequent chats with Keegan, I just wished he would get on with playing and leave coaching to the management. He would lose the players if he carried on that way, and if he wanted a bit of extra training with Darren, Jon, me, or whoever, that would not have been a problem. But he seemed to be pre-arranging coaching sessions with the manager. I think Ali knew he was the daddy, but had become a little bit too comfortable and lost some of his focus.

We lost our next game 2–0 at Southampton and although it may not seem a particularly significant result in the history of the club it was the day I believe Keegan finally lost the dressing room. We were booed off by our own fans and I remained on the bench that day. In the dressing room, however, views were

WHO LET THE GOAT OUT?

expressed about which the supporters would have known nothing. It was a Keegan team that played that day, with the exception of Kevin Horlock, Shaun Wright-Phillips and Richard Dunne, and I wondered who he would point the finger at.

Wrighty had been the only one running around and trying his heart out, and because I was not playing I waited to see what he would say.

The next match we played was against Chelsea, and I started up front with Anelka. I remember in the first few minutes being in on goal and Marcel Desailly pulling me back just outside the box when I only had the keeper to beat. It was a clear red card and the fans were going mad, but Dermot Gallagher only showed him a yellow. We lost the game 3–0, but at least I had temporarily won back my place in the starting line-up. We beat Birmingham 2–0 away and then I scored at West Bromwich in a 2–1 win (as well as missing a sitter!). Although I was not aware of it at the time, that was my ninety-eighth goal for City. The next league game on 9 November 2002 was at home to Manchester United. I crossed my fingers that I would finally get to start against the team that had brought me to England, having been on the bench for my previous two matches against them. I half expected not to play, and avoided getting too excited about the prospect – I had been there before.

We lost the midweek League Cup tie at Wigan 1–0, but I was relieved to see my name next to Anelka's on the team sheet for the Manchester derby. At last I had a chance to show Fergie what I could do, and I knew that if I put up a good performance in this game Keegan would have to stick with me.

It was the last Maine Road derby ever so we knew we had to beat United for our fans, but we had our work cut out. Lucien Mettomo and Gerard Wiekens replaced Distin and Steve Howey who were both absent, and we started as underdogs. I had studied

United and knew that if I scored against them it would be best not to get over-excited because they had a habit of coming back. To remain calm until we were certain of a victory was the best approach. It felt good to be on the stage in front of our supporters; this was the opportunity I had been waiting for. I was upset that David Beckham and Roy Keane were out, because if we beat them I wanted us to beat them all and United not to be able to make up excuses.

This game, for me, showed the true quality of Gerard Wiekens. Whenever he was called upon to do a job he did it superbly – in fact, whenever he marked me in training I always had a difficult time. On this day he marked Ruud van Nistelrooy as well as I have seen anyone do. Gerard was not the quickest, but he read the game well and that day he did not allow Ruud a sniff.

I had watched Ruud's game over a couple of seasons and come to the conclusion that our games were not a million miles apart. Neither of us seemed to get many – if any – goals outside the box, and the fact that Gerard marked Ruud as well as he did me proved we had a similar style. Every time Ruud made a move, Gerard had him in shackles, as if to say, 'I've got you – you're not going anywhere'.

I was very relaxed as we kicked off. Anelka scored an early goal to put us 1–0 up but Paul Scholes soon made it 1–1. It was a fast, exciting game, but when Marc Vivien Foe played a long ball up front he miscued it and it was heading out for a goal kick. As the ball rolled towards the line I thought, 'I could make this bad ball into a good ball.' Gary Neville seemed to be trying to shepherd the ball out as I chased him down, and I could see the ball was going out. I expected him to shield it as I challenged him, but then he decided to play it back to Fabien Barthez. I anticipated his next move and put in a block tackle and the ball stayed in play. I edged him out of the way, took the ball in towards goal, but there was

138

nobody for me to square the ball to. I was on my own, so I went along the goal line and tried to angle back in a little before hitting the ball low past Barthez and into the net. While the fans went hysterical, I stuck to my guns and avoided getting too excited, because United had plenty more left and were not about to roll over. I had seen enough teams fall into the trap of thinking the game was won, and end up losing.

We were playing well and I was feeling good, all the time thinking, 'Now they're going to see the real Shaun Goater'. I was up against Laurent Blanc and Rio Ferdinand – and I found the game very easy. I was spinning off them, laying balls out wide or into Eyal, and then letting him take over. We went in 2–1 up, at which point I heard 'Feed the Goat!' at its loudest ever. The fans had also come up with a new song, 'Who let the Goat out?' and I thought, 'I'm having that one!' I liked the tune and it reminded me of summer in Bermuda, so I was very happy with the City fans' latest release! Early in the second half Eyal picked up the ball in the middle, and as I ran infield I saw a gap behind the defenders and began to sprint into it, knowing Eyal would find me. He played a perfectly weighted pass into my stride. I had to hold off two defenders, but delayed my shot until I drew closer and closer to goal. Choosing the right moment to pull the trigger would be key, and having studied United I knew Barthez's habits as a sharp and agile keeper. If you hit the ball in low he had the ability to make some fantastic saves. Knowing that his strength lay in low shots I had always thought that if I ever was one-on-one with him, I'd dink it over him. As I held off the defenders the ball bounced in front of me, allowing me to make a gentle half-volley over Barthez, who had gambled on the low shot. The ball gently bounced into the back of the net. That was 3–1 and also turned out to be my hundredth goal for the club, although I didn't know it at the time. I ran off to the United fans saying, 'Ssshhh! I can't hear you any more!' I celebrated that goal a bit more than the first one, but I still wanted to remain cautious, there still being quite a bit of time left.

I had waited so long for this moment against United, who represented a yardstick in English football as far as I was concerned. As a youngster in Bermuda this had been the team I wanted to play against because they were the team to beat. Today it may be Chelsea – but back then it was United.

We held out comfortably to win 3–1 and I walked off to an incredible rendition of 'Feed the Goat' followed by 'Who let the Goat out?' What an amazing way to end a fantastic day. This was the first time that City had beaten United in thirteen years. We had taken 4 points off United that season, and I did wonder if that made a difference to their title challenge. I was really pleased for Gerard, too, because he had played magnificently and he deserved all the plaudits that came his way. Gerard had the same attitude as I, in that he always did his best when he came into the side and accepted being left out with a good grace, even if he was not happy about it. The whole team played really well that day. All I wanted now was a shirt, and I didn't mind whose I got – they were all good players. I did like Scholes because he was an England international and kept a low profile, but I got a rejection when one of our security guys went and enquired in their dressing room – 'It's all packed away', he was told.

I walked up to Keegan's room near the tunnel and Ferguson was in there. I asked him how he was doing, and whether there was any chance I could get Scholes's shirt. I think I was treated to what is now commonly known as the hairdryer treatment from the Reds' boss. I was glad I had scored against his team that day and my only regret was that I did not have the chance to ask him to sign the match-ball too, but two goals were good enough. Somebody mentioned to me that the only person who had scored three goals against United that season was Ronaldo in the Champions League game. I left empty-handed but not too bothered. It was a proud day for me and my family and as I drove home I thought that surely now I had won Keegan over. He did not say anything special to me after the game and my 'Well done' was no different from anyone else's. What I didn't know was that I'd won a Man of the Match award from one of our main sponsors, who wanted to present a glass boot in an interview later. Keegan was too busy to participate and the award was given to me a few months afterwards in a box after training. Maybe it was cluttering up Keegan's office?

CHAPTER FIFTEEN

Keegan Gets His Wish

I remained in the team for the next seven games and although I worked hard my only reward was one goal at Sunderland, so it was no surprise when I was dropped for the trip to Fulham over Christmas. I had had the run I craved but had chosen a rotten time to hit a dry spell. One thing that made me smile during that barren run was yet another new song from the supporters – even though I initially thought it was aimed at a teammate. I am not sure which game it was, but as we came in at half-time I heard what I thought to be 'Come on feed the Foe, come on feed the Foe, he wants more, more, more!' I said to Marc, 'Did you hear that? They're singing a song about you – that's an awesome tune', and I carried on singing it to Marc, who was smiling away. Then a few of the lads said, 'It's about you, Goat – they're singing "Come on feed the Goat"' – and it turned out to be true. I was made up with it – a third killer song to add to the collection and a greatest hits album in the offing.

I was left on the bench for the following two games as well, but Hucks did not score in my absence and I was very surprised to be recalled for the 2–1 win over Terry Venables's Leeds in which I scored and Niclas Jensen volleyed home an incredible second. That was a weird game because everyone was aware that Keegan was chasing Leeds striker Robbie Fowler. I thought there was every chance he would sign, and that if he did I would have to concede that my future probably lay elsewhere. Eyal Berkovic and Marc Vivien Foe clearly thought so too, as they shook my hand as I left the pitch. Keegan wanted to play his signings ahead of me and the whole situation was starting to become a drain on my confidence. I was still eager to prove him wrong and show him that I was an asset to the team, but I was not sure how long I could go on like that. It was funny, because when we played at Newcastle the following week I missed a good chance and the Newcastle fans started singing 'One Robbie Fowler, there's only one Robbie Fowler' to me, even though he still hadn't signed. I smiled at it, because I always took that kind of thing to be a challenge, which of course I thrived on. What I did not know was that it would be the last occasion I would start in City's first team, apart from the final game of the season.

Robbie was a player whom I admired greatly and I thought that so long as I could challenge him and have a chance of playing it was fine by me, because he was an awesome striker. I just wanted to know that I was in with a shout. I recalled a time I had played against him in a friendly and had asked before the match if I could swap shirts, but he gave the old line that he couldn't give it out because the Liverpool kit man would not allow it. Paul Dickov had overheard it all and come up smiling, making gestures to suggest that I had been given a custard pie in the face – I had been pied, all right. He finally signed, after initially pulling out of the deal, and when he met the lads I reminded him of that day, saying, 'I asked you for your shirt, you wouldn't give it me and now you want to come here and take my shirt?' It was a joke meant to help him settle in, but Robbie claimed he could not remember the occasion. I felt that my form still was not that bad, but that Keegan mismanaged things from then on. He had a new striker who clearly was not fit and he made a statement saying as much to the press, so it made no sense that he had a fully fit striker who was desperate to play and did not use me. If he had played me for seventy minutes or so for the first half-dozen games and then eased Robbie in as substitute until he was fully fit, surely that would have been of more benefit to both the team and Robbie, who was perhaps 70 per cent fit. He could have come on, built up his fitness and showed a few glimpses of what he was capable of, instead of being under intense pressure to score from the first game. Had Keegan done that he would not have lost me mentally and physically. Playing someone not much more than half-fit was tantamount to saying, 'Thanks very much, but we don't need you any more'. He continued playing Robbie, giving the excuse that he was not fit yet, and it was five games before he found the net. During that time I scored what would prove to be my last goal for City.

I had now resigned myself to leaving City in order to play regular first-team football again, even though it would be a massive wrench and was the last thing I wanted to do. It was business as usual at Old Trafford as we played the return fixture with United and I was back on the bench. The derby at Maine Road, just a few months earlier, seemed a long time ago and my hope of consistently playing against United was fading away. I was fairly relaxed, knowing that at best I was going to be on the bench from now on, but I was still desperate for us to win. We were 1–0 down and I began to think that if I was given twenty minutes I could do something because I had no fear of them. The clock ticked away and by the time we entered the last ten I was just fed up, because I was not going to have much time to change anything. It was a case of déjà vu, as I had had virtually the same experience under Joe Royle two years earlier. I eventually came on, along with Ali Benarbia and Wrighty and within six seconds I got on the end of Ali's free kick to head home the equaliser, the quickest goal by a substitute in Premiership history, I believe. I had planned to copy an Eric Cantona celebration in front of the United fans if I did come on and score, but did not get the chance because the lads were on me within a second. 'Get off me – you're ruining my celebration!' I protested internally. A few minutes later Wrighty hit the bar, Anelka picked up the rebound, squared it to me and I swept the ball home, but the referee, Alan Wiley, disallowed it for handball against Nicolas. Still, I had finally scored at Old Trafford and it was awesome to hear the City fans shouting my name and it echoing around the ground as we walked off the park.

I was an unused substitute for our next game, at home to Arsenal, and I tried to keep my spirits up by having the occasional laugh with the lads in the dressing room. 'Look guys,' I said, 'if you score today, I've got a T-shirt I'm going to wear under my top with "va-va-voom" on it, so run to me if you score.' It was a little mickey-take of Thierry Henry's Renault advert of the time and the guys were all up for it. But within just twenty minutes Henry had torn us apart and we were 4–0 down, and the other lads on the bench were looking at me as if to say, 'I don't think you'll be using that shirt today, Goat'. At half-time I ran up the tunnel and ripped it off and threw it in the bin, but as the lads went out after the break they were still asking me if I had it on. I asked them whether they were serious. 'We're losing four bloody nil!' I reminded them. Whether he knew it or not, Thierry Henry definitely got one over on us that day. I was making the odd appearance as substitute here and there even though we had only scored twice in six league games since the draw at United. With five games to go there were a few suggestions in the press that I might be named captain for the last game at Maine Road, but I was not certain of it until a few days before the game. People were coming up to me and asking whether it was true. I would tell them I did not know and the general reaction was, 'Well you better bloody had be captain!' I had no indication from Keegan at that point, however.

I still had a year on my contract, but despite all my efforts to impress the manager I had accepted that it was futile and it would be best if I moved on. There was no announcement as such, but everyone assumed that my last game for City would coincide with the club's last game at Maine Road. If it all happened and I was skipper for the day, that would be quite a send-off.

I trained and continued to put everything into each session, and I was still enjoying working with Juan Osorio, who kept his fitness sessions interesting and varied. He was an excellent coach and I remember Sky Sports wanted to do an interview with him. Juan was still way ahead of the game with his methods. He travelled all round the world in search of new techniques and to learn from the very best in his field. I thought it was great that Sky wanted to do a feature on his work because he deserved some recognition for what he was doing. I had spoken with Stuart Pearce about Juan and asked if he had ever come across his style of coaching before, bearing in mind that Stuart had played at the top for almost twenty years. He said he had not, and that he thought it was really good stuff and he would ask Juan for notes on some of his sessions because he was heading down the path of coaching himself – quite a compliment.

It was announced that the Southampton game would be my farewell appearance and that everybody was happy with everything, but Keegan wanted a fee for me so when fans asked me who I was signing for I would just say, 'I ain't going

anywhere!' I still had a year left and although I had accepted I had
to move on, if nothing materialised during the summer I would be
back for pre-season training in July. I had not spoken to anyone
and had not been told I could leave on a free transfer. I had had the
best years of my life with City and was not going to let this spoil
my memories of playing for the club. Finally it was confirmed that
I would captain the side for the last game, and from then on I had
to prepare mentally so that I would give a good performance on
the day, especially with it being Maine Road's last game. The fact
that it might be my last game for City was secondary so far as I
was concerned, and I thought as any fan might and wondered
what memento I could take away with me from the ground on that
day! I was hoping to get the 'Home Team' sign off the changing
room door, if I could get a screwdriver from somebody.

Knowing the historic importance of the day, I left earlier than
usual for Maine Road. It was typical Mancunian weather, grey
skies and light drizzle, as I turned off a side street towards the
ground. It was only when I arrived in the car park that I realised
that a lot of supporters were treating this not only as Maine Road's
last game but as a Shaun Goater day too. No sooner had I turned
off the engine than about a hundred people swarmed around my
car. Security came over to make sure I was okay and it took me
about forty-five minutes to walk 50 yards to the players' entrance
as I tried to write my name on what felt like several hundred bits
of paper and other items that were pushed towards me by fans
wanting me to sign anything and everything. I would write an 'S'
on one bit of paper, an 'h' on another, and so on. Anita settled the
girls and started filming everything. Looking back at the tape, it is
unbelievable. As I neared the entrance the fans started singing my
name and it was an incredible start to what would be a very
emotional day. Whatever was happening regarding my future, it
was clear that so far as the people I had met outside were

concerned this was my last game for City, and their last chance to get an autograph or to wish me well.

Once inside I must admit I felt a little drained physically and emotionally, which was not ideal because if this was to be my final appearance I wanted to go out on a high. I had to do my best to put the past hour out of my mind and focus on the game ahead. One thing was for sure; this was an occasion when nobody was going to mess up my day. There was nothing anyone could do to spoil it for me, and I was totally buzzing and happy. Keegan announced the team and said that I was going to be captain, and I felt really proud and honoured to be the man leading City out for the final game at Maine Road. I also decided that I was not going to lose the captaincy band – they would have to rip it off my arm if they wanted it back. The boys were great and all came up, patting me on the back and wishing me all the best. I wanted to go out and give one last really good performance, and badly wanted to win the game so that I could sign off on a personal high; and, more importantly, so we could give the old stadium a rousing send-off.

As we warmed up on the pitch for a few minutes Robbie Fowler and I were doing stretches near to one another and Robbie looked around the ground, which was still filling up, and said, 'These people love you, don't they Shaun? I'd give anything for a bit of this.' This was Robbie Fowler – one of the most revered strikers in Europe, saying he was taken aback by the way the City fans were with me – boy, did that feel good! I raised my eyebrows, feeling even prouder and a few feet taller because, to me, that was a real pat on the back. I told Robbie that he did have the same kind of adulation at Liverpool, where they still worshipped him (little did I know he would experience it again in a couple of years!). As I went back down the tunnel, I looked forward to my last ninety minutes at Maine Road.

Finally, it was time to come out, and as we walked down the tunnel we were hit by a wall of noise and a sea of banners and flags; and there were so many with my name on that I was stunned. There were so many saying things like 'Legend' and 'We love you Shaun', and my favourite – a flag with 'All I need is the air that I breathe and Shaun Goater' – fantastic! I had expected them to be all about Maine Road and it hit home even harder as I thought, 'Hell! These fans really think the world of me'. This was Maine Road's day, but the fans seemed intent on making it into a special day for me, too. As the names were read out I was very conscious about mine being called, and before it was, the fans broke out into a chorus of 'Feed the Goat', followed by 'Blue Moon'. The hairs on the back of my neck stood up. There was an amazing reception just for the announcement of my name: the feeling was so fantastic, like a dream you never want to end. Then I tossed the coin and we got into the game, but I was mentally drained by the occasion and also knew that Southampton were there to spoil the party. I would do the same thing in their shoes; I would not want just to turn up and roll over so that everyone could enjoy themselves, I would want to ruin it by scoring and winning the game. We were both mid-table and I think eighth place was up for grabs in terms of something to play for other than the history of the day. But of course we had to win. They were more relaxed than we were, and the emotion of the day certainly got to me. At half-time we were 1–0 down and in the dressing room Keegan told me that he did not care if it was my last game and added, 'If you don't buck your ideas up you're coming off in five minutes!'

I cannot recall whether I had actually done enough to warrant the tirade, but when he had finished the lads came up to me, saying that he was wrong to do that and they thought I was not playing that badly. But I was okay, because I was determined there was no way Keegan could upset me today – I would not allow him or anyone else to do so. In fairness to Keegan, I think he was just trying to put across how important it was for us to win the game, but we all knew that and felt the same way as he did. As it was, after about fifteen minutes of the second half he brought me off and put Robbie on, but although I was disappointed to come off earlier than I had expected to, I still did not feel for certain that this was going to be my last game for City because everything was still up in the air.

The standing ovation I received from all four corners of the ground – even the Southampton fans – proved that so far as the fans were concerned I would be leaving the club in the summer. It was truly breathtaking, awesome – call it what you will – but I was humbled by it. I thought of all the highs and lows I had experienced at Maine Road and I can honestly say that, despite the result and having to come off when I did, I still enjoyed every minute of that day, from the moment I got out of my car on arrival.

The walk around Maine Road after the final whistle was just as emotional and all the lads enjoyed the moment and soaked up as much of the atmosphere and the occasion as possible. The passion I felt from those fans was tangible and I could not and did not want to imagine that I would never play in front of them again.

Afterwards I went up to one of the hospitality rooms where my family and a few of our friends were – Julie England, Simon Barker, Keith Pinner and a few others. They told me that there were a couple of hundred fans outside and they would not leave until I came out to see them. Our friends had made plans for us to go to a nice, quiet restaurant in town, and we wanted to go home and get changed for dinner. Normally going out after a match was the last thing Anita and I wanted to do because we preferred to go home, rest up and have a family dinner, but of course this was a special occasion and we were happy to go along with it. We said our goodbyes and when we reached the main entrance there must have been about 400 people waiting in the pouring rain. My car was brought up to the door, but those drenched fans were singing 'Feed the Goat' and I was not going to leave without thanking them first.

I went to the barricades and began giving everyone hugs and kisses goodbye, as well as signing whatever they wanted signed, but most had stuff that was soaked and soggy so it was not easy. It was so amazing that they had waited for me in such appalling weather. It said everything about what they thought of me, and I was staggered.

I was out there for about fifteen minutes – soaked through as well by now – before getting into the car with Anita and the girls. I had to edge out slowly because there were people all around us. Finally I got out onto the road and began to drive away.

As I turned the corner I stopped at a pedestrian crossing outside the Parkside pub and suddenly people began rushing over to the car and coming out of the pub, surrounding us, banging on the car and shouting, 'We love you! Don't go Shaun – stay at City!' It was brilliant. It was a rough pub, but these guys only had good intentions. Anita made sure that the girls, now aged three, were settled and understood what was happening. I thanked everyone, told them how much it all meant to me, and then we crawled away because by this time we were holding up a lot of traffic.

When we turned on to the dual carriageway there was more cheering and beeping of horns as people spotted our car. It was an incredible journey home and when we finally parked at the house I turned off the engine and Anita and I both took a deep breath, hardly able to take it all in. I asked, 'You got all that on tape, right?' – and she had.

We had a sitter to look after the girls and went back to Maine Road to pick up our friends, who had remained at the ground. Julie England staggered out with a toilet seat from the home dressing room and said, 'I've got my memento – just think, all the top players have had their ass on this at some point!' It didn't bear thinking about . . .

We were in a cab and drove into Manchester but what we did not know was that the restaurant we were headed to, Rafa's, was anything but quiet. As we walked through the door we saw about 200 City fans, who started cheering and singing as soon as they saw us. I just looked at my friends Keith and his daughter Julie and nodded to them – they had got me, hook, line and sinker, and I felt as though I was on the end of a schoolboy prank. They just laughed and said that this was where I belonged, and they certainly had a point. From the moment we sat down until about 1am, the fans, often orchestrated by former City star Gary Owen, were singing songs about City and me, and at one point they sang 'One Mrs Goater – there's only one Mrs Goater!' Anita finally got a taste of what it was like. And to think that these supporters had not even liked me for my first eighteen months at the club. It was an awesome, awesome night – and what a great night to end a great day.

Not long afterwards we set off for Bermuda for our summer break, but I still did not know where I would be playing next season. The club wanted a fee and I was not sure who, if anyone, would come in for me. There would be a few twists and turns before I finally left City.

CHAPTER SIXTEEN

A Member of the Royal Family

I was outside my house with the twins back in Bermuda, pottering around the garden, and I kept popping inside to watch bits of the Cameroon versus Colombia match in Paris. Marc Vivien Foe was playing and I wanted to see how he was doing. One time when I went in to watch, the commentator was saying that Marc had collapsed and was being treated by the medical team. The TV shots showed the players and supporters, but there were none of Marc and nobody knew whether he had fainted or was suffering from heat exhaustion. Within about half an hour the news filtered through that Marc had died. I could not believe it; I was totally numb. Like everyone else, I wanted to know the reason why a footballer in the prime of his life had died so suddenly.

The whole squad attended his funeral in France and not long afterwards we began our pre-season training. Marc's death, caused by a virtually undetectable heart condition, did not really hit me until we went back inside to get changed in the Carrington dressing rooms. The area by the sink, where Marc always sat, was empty. He used to move the water bottles off the drainer, then sit there, leaning back against the mirror and discussing training or whatever. I always changed close to the sink area and I now looked up to where he used to sit and it was strange not to see him there. Then, more than ever, I realised that we were never going to see him again. Looking at Marc, because of his size you would have thought that if he became angry he could just steam through players, but you would be wrong. He was one of the most gentle men you could ever have met. His game was neat and tidy; he would win it or receive the ball, control it and lay it off. He was very strong, did not clatter people or leave his foot in. He would arrive at Carrington in any number of colourful outfits; some of the bright yellows and reds he wore would have looked loud even in Bermuda! His trainers were so bright they might as well have had alarm bells fitted to them, they made so much noise.

But he was so kind and considerate, and he never had a go at anybody or tried to make them look small. Even if he got any stick he would just take it, then go and try to prove otherwise on the pitch. He was a team player who played only for the team; he never spoke about anyone behind his back or criticised anyone, and he was a terrific person simply because of the way he was. With Marc, what you saw was what you got and he is still very much missed by everyone at the club and around the world.

The summer of 2003 proved a very eventful one. While relaxing at home, I received a call from the Governor's secretary in Bermuda asking if I would accept an MBE. The first thing I did was check it really was the Governor's secretary and then, when I'd ascertained this, I said 'Yes, of course I'd accept an MBE' – all the while I'm thinking 'What the hell is an MBE?' I knew it was something awarded to people in different industries for services to others but I had to look it up on the Internet to find exactly what it was all about – thank God for the Internet!

After I'd done a little bit of research, my next question was 'What for?' I needed to find out why I was being awarded this honour, and the Governor's secretary explained it was for services to the youth of Bermuda over a period of time. I thought that was really nice, but it wasn't the reason I'd been organising soccer camps and suchlike since 1992 – I never set out earn an MBE, if that makes any sense, but I was honoured to be selected all the same. I think it was a mix of the football and being seen as an ambassador for my country in England. All I had to do now was choose where to receive my award – Governor's House in Bermuda or Buckingham Palace. The funny thing about that is, when I was around 12 I lived in Marsh Folly and my house ran along the boundary of the Governor's House, so there'd been many occasions when I'd climbed over the wall, then a fence and then another wall to get into the grounds before being chased off by some irate security guard. Now I was being invited to accept an MBE in the Governor's house; things had certainly come full circle and if I had chosen to accept it there, I reckon I'd have had to climb over those walls again, just for old times' sake!

Of course, it had to be Buckingham Palace because it meant a chance to meet the Queen or Prince Charles and it would be an unforgettable occasion. It would give Anita and my mum the chance to get a nice frock, too, so we headed for the capital on 10 December 2003. My mum was her usual down-to-earth self and she flew over for a few days to go to the Palace. 'You don't need to buy me a new dress or anything,' my mum told me and I had to smile. 'Mum, we've got to get you all decked out,' I told her. 'Big hat, the works!' She was more bothered about the day interrupting a game! I explained there was no match and even if there had been, I wouldn't have been playing.

We lived about 50 minutes from London so weren't unduly concerned about rushing – hey, we're Bermudian, right? We were the last to arrive! We sheepishly took our seats at the back and caught a discerning glance from the host: 'Now that everyone is here . . .' Anita whispered that it was typical of us not to allow for heavy traffic. Jonny Wilkinson was there that day too, and all the media were swarming around him because he was the man of the moment and many believed he would surpass David Beckham's fame at that point. We were taken through all the protocol about what you can and can't do when you meet the Queen, and shortly before I collected my MBE I saw Jonny ahead of me so I took the opportunity of congratulating him on his achievements. He looked at me and said, 'It's Goater isn't it?' I said 'Yeah' then thought 'How the bloody hell does he know who I am?' He answered it himself when he said 'Will Greenwood goes bloody mental about you!' Will was a big City fan but it threw me a little so I told Jonny to say hello to Will for me and to keep up the good work. Jonny asked me not to run off afterwards because he had a relative in the car who was a huge City fan and they'd love to get my autograph. I said no problem and asked if I could get his. He said he had a better idea and that he'd sign his tie and give it to me if I'd sign mine and give it to him. I would actually miss him after the ceremony because of the media scrum and Anita and my mum admiring the Palace loos, but we exchanged ties through the post at a later date and that's something I'll keep – it won't be appearing on eBay!

I was nervous about receiving the MBE from the Queen because I thought I was bound to get something wrong. You're not really supposed to engage the Queen in small talk but, me being me, I had one burning question I needed an answer to and as I went up to her I said, 'You'll have to tell me, are you a Red or a Blue?' She told me she supported everyone, and I said 'Come on,

156

you can tell me,' but she just smiled, shook my hand and slightly pushed my hand away – it's the Queen's way of saying that while it's been nice meeting you, 'Do one!' I thanked her and went out for the photographs and a few quotes outside and watched Jonny receiving his award on the TV. Quite an occasion . . .

Returning to the uncertainty of my future, I would learn of interest from another club in, shall we say, unusual circumstances. I made it my business to check out any clubs that ever showed an interest in signing me. I would research the club, its stability, its financial situation, the qualities of the players and whether they included any individuals who could benefit me and help me develop. I had done this at Bristol and I was fortunate enough to have already known Manchester City before I signed for the club. Now I had to do it again.

After Marc's funeral I returned to Carrington for training in July having had no firm offers presented through my agent during the close season. A lot of the lads were saying things like 'What are you still doing here?' A few asked how I could have had such a great send-off and still be at the club, but it was all tongue-in-cheek. Keegan was fine with me and he knew I had to report for training because I still had a year left on my contract.

I was certain I would be moving on and I needed to keep fit in order to be in shape for my next club. I played a small role in a couple of pre-season friendlies, which baffled the City fans too, although they were as good with me as they always had been. It was the fee that was a stumbling block for a number of clubs, although the fans could not have been aware of that.

The first I learned of any interest from another club was when I was queuing at the check-in at Manchester airport for City's tour of Denmark. Keegan told me that Reading had come in for me and that I should talk with them right away. I did not want to be rushed into anything and still wanted to build my fitness up, so I said that I would travel with the squad. 'Well, I'm not planning to play you in any of the games', said Keegan, but I went anyway. This move had to be right for Shaun Goater and his family.

A week after we had returned to England I went to talk with Reading. I had done my homework on Alan Pardew, an up-and-coming young manager, and knew they had a solid chairman in John Madejski. They had a terrific stadium, excellent training facilities and a good squad, so they were ticking all the right boxes. But Nottingham Forest and Wigan had also shown strong interest, and I told Reading that I would be speaking with them, too. I wanted to hear what each club had to say, why each felt it would be the best club for me probably to end my career with. Sunderland had expressed an interest but were unable to afford the fee, and even Mark McGhee at Millwall made an enquiry, which I found surprising.

I asked Paul Hart at Forest whether the club would be selling any of their talented players because I knew they were struggling financially. Hart could not guarantee they would not be cashing in one or two, and that convinced me that moving there would not be a particularly good idea. I enjoyed speaking with Paul Jewell and his chairman Dave Whelan at Wigan. Jewell was brilliant and Whelan said to me, 'This is what we're offering – a three-year deal, no negotiating, take it or leave it'. I respected his honesty but felt they were relying on the fact that I lived in the north-west and would not want to uproot my family. I did not feel it was the right move for me. Then Rupert Lowe at Southampton called my agent to see what was happening and express his interest. He asked Mark to tell me 'not to make any rash decisions'.

Ultimately, though, Reading was the club that most appealed to me. After an exhausting medical I signed a three-year contract and City received £500,000 for me (a percentage of which went to Bristol City) – a £100,000 profit, no less. Chairman/owner John

Madejski claimed that I was the biggest signing in Reading's history, and added that it was a psychological blow to every other club in the division. I knew I would never be in a position where the club could not pay my wages and although I was not on anything like what I had earned with City, within a few days of working with Pardew on the training pitch I felt I had made the right choice. Everyone I spoke to told me that he was a promising manager and they all proved correct. Within six weeks of starting work with him I had learned more tactically than I had done in my previous fourteen years in England.

Pardew, who told me he wanted to build the team round me, would take a session and say, 'This is what it will be like for the first twenty minutes'; then he would do another session telling us, 'This is how it will be after sixty minutes', and more often than not he was spot on – that was exactly how it turned out during the match. He would line us up to defend a free kick and tell us to squeeze the opposition out; as the kick was taken we had somebody designated to shout out a trigger name and when we heard it we knew that we would all rush out at the last second to catch them offside. Some people watching might think it is a spur of the moment thing, but with Pardew it was a well-drilled, well-executed and successful defence.

It felt strange to be at another club after investing so much emotion and hard work at City, but I was happy enough with Reading and began with a goal in my third game. I then went on to four goals in six games, so I hit the ground running, as I tried to do at all the clubs for which I had played.

Then the whispers started about West Ham being interested in Pardew filling the managerial vacancy at Upton Park. My first thought was that West Ham fans were similar to City supporters and would be expecting a big name to take the reins. I felt there was little chance West Ham would take Pardew on because he was relatively unknown at the top level and would have his work cut out from the word go. I knew he had the credentials to do really well as time went on, because he was fresh and hungry. Obviously West Ham's board felt the same because they came in for him. 'Please don't go', I thought to myself. He was one of the main reasons I had gone to Reading and he was leaving *already*? This was the first sign that things might not go the way I had hoped with the Royals. Ultimately I would need to move on again in search of first-team football.

Everything seemed to be geared around Nicky Forster at Reading. He was a fair player with plenty of pace, but not a fantastic return in terms of goals. I wondered why the fans liked him so much because he averaged one every three or four games. I worked out that it was because it was a long time since they had had a prolific goalscorer and Forster was the nearest thing they had. If they were happy with his goal ratio, they might really take to me if I could keep my career average of one in every two games. When I actually played alongside Forster I had some difficulties with his style of play. He would get into some great positions and was not unlike Darren Huckerby in many ways, but Darren was cleverer in his selection of shots and passes. Forster would take out two or three defenders, create space for me, but continually shoot from impossible angles. I had been warned that he would be frustrating to play with, and so it proved in my first couple of games. In my third match Pardew said to Forster, 'If you get into those positions again and don't lay the ball off, you won't play for this team'. He added that he thought he was a great player with all the attributes to be a real asset to the side and then added, 'But if you've got someone square and you try and shoot from the byeline when there's somebody waiting for a tap-in again, I won't play you.' I listened to all this and thought 'We're gonna be successful', because for partnerships to work you have to look for your teammate and if he is better placed, you lay it off to him. That was what I would do every time.

A couple of games later Pardew was gone. I am certain that if he had stayed we would have gone up, because we had flown off the blocks and would have taken some stopping. We had also had a manager who was not afraid to tackle potential problems early on, but of course he went and that was the end of that.

Kevin Dillon took over for about six games and we could not find a win to save our lives. Pardew left a huge hole because he had been involved in every aspect of the club, from running the first team to making the tea ladies smile. He had wanted to be in charge of a happy crew, and as its leader he took it upon himself to make a connection with everybody. Dillon told us he wanted the job and asked us to carry on the work Pardew had started, but it just didn't happen. Forster went back to his old ways and we were suddenly going backwards again. We were in tenth place when Steve Coppell took over. I decided to go and see him once he had settled in at the club – a move I later believed might have been a bad decision.

First of all I asked him what he looked for in his strikers and – clever Coppell – he called up about every attribute you could think of. Good link-up play, creativity; just about everything I thought I couldn't do! I then told him I thought we had a really good chance of going up, adding that I thought Nicky Forster was the player who held the key. I told him that if he could get Forster to know when to do it for himself and when to do it for the team, we would be all right.

Forster was the club's king but his goal ratio did not back that up, and I wondered why we were all playing to his beat. All that was needed was for someone to say that he was important to the team but needed to change his game slightly – if he did, he would benefit the team even more and score more himself. But Pardew remained the only man to have told him where he was going wrong.

As a result, I ended the season as top scorer with fourteen goals – my lowest tally against games played since my Rotherham days. I was really disappointed at that, plus we had just missed out on the play-offs and had to watch as Pardew's West Ham lost to Crystal Palace in the play-off final. (West Ham were promoted in the following year's play-off final.) It was a poor season for me in terms of goals, but with two more years on my contract I knew there was time to be part of a successful Reading side.

Part of our pre-season included a game against City at the Madejski Stadium with the profits going to my Grass Roots programme in Bermuda, and I owe heartfelt thanks to Kevin Keegan, to City and to Reading for this match. The idea behind Grass Roots was making the odds a bit more favourable for another Bermuda kid to make it in England or anywhere in the world. The programme is aimed at developing the youngsters through a higher level of coaching and I had set it up after discussions with certain people at City who knew what should and should not be done.

I had been involved in soccer camps since 1992 when David Bascome and I had begun the Bascome/Goater Pro-Soccer programme through my experiences in English football. Having seen the successful youth programmes in England at close quarters we were keen to pass on our knowledge and professionalism to Bermudian kids. We thought we could eventually develop it into a business by getting sponsors on board and taking it out to schools and youth or community groups. Initially we charged the kids $5, which we gave back to them in the form of T-shirts. We ran it like that until 1998, when the Bank of Bermuda became our main sponsor and it turned out that we would be getting more funds than the Bermuda FA! We could invest the money into the programme because it was professionally run with structure and planning, and the kids and their parents were happy. I wanted to change the dates of the camp because it clashed with my pre-season training but David was concerned the bank might pull out if we altered anything, so I told him I was happy for him to continue running it and keep my name associated with it, though it is now called the Bank of Bermuda Pro-Soccer camp. I could start another programme run along lines other than discipline and coaching. And so Grass Roots was born. Based around entertainment and enjoyment, it was free for kids to take part in and run by volunteers. My intention was to invite professional clubs over to assist with coaching the youngsters, and City came over three years running until 2005. That really put us on the map.

The reason for City coming for the first three years was so that the coaching staff could understand Bermuda football standards, people and facilities. They could then deliver an informed opinion on whether a pro-league was feasible for Bermuda. David and I wrote up a plan to start a pro five-a-side league in 1996, but as we were both concentrating on our careers we left the venture on the back burner until our careers ended. Now that I had moved to Reading, part of the deal I agreed was that City would play us in a pre-season friendly to help raise funds for the next trip. Of course the City fans did not let me down and more than 4,000 travelled down for a game that was watched by a crowd of 11,586. It was wonderful to run out and see that so many had come to watch the game and to hear the original rendition of 'Feed the Goat'. Some of the Reading lads were a bit taken aback by the backing the City fans were giving me, saying that they knew I had been popular at City but had not realised quite how much they thought of me. City gave us quite a beating on the night, winning 4–1 and making it seem so easy with their movement and slick passing, but at least we made £39,000 towards Grass Roots. It was a great run out and I enjoyed the evening thoroughly. It was also the only time I ever played against City at senior level – although I never played against them in a competitive game for any club.

I started the season on the bench. Coppell told me he was going to go with Dave Kitson and Nicky Forster for the first ten games and see how it panned out. I felt I should be starting, but there was no point kicking up a fuss, I had to respect the decision. As it happened the new partnership did not really work, but Coppell had made it clear he was not going to change anything until ten games had passed. Kitson and Forster scored ten times between them during that time and Coppell did try a different combination before the tenth game, but not one involving me. I had to wait until October for my first start in a League Cup tie with Oxford, in which I scored; but I was dropped the next game. I began to feel that I had been here before. Up to the end of November I had around four starts, but the thing that really angered me was when I was denied playing for Bermuda unnecessarily.

Kyle Lightbourne was the new national coach of Bermuda and had selected me to play, and as I was not playing for Reading I thought I might as well go home and play for my country. I told Kyle I would not let him down but before my departure Dave Kitson picked up an injury and Kevin Dillon persuaded me to stay at Reading because I was set to be his replacement. This was a chance to show Coppell what I had, and I was given assurances I would definitely play on the Saturday. I had to call Kyle and tell him I could not come because of the situation at my club and he accepted it with his usual good grace. The Bermuda press was not so happy and I received a bit of a slating in the papers for not travelling home and for putting Reading first. It was the first time I had had any negative press back home and it felt a little uncomfortable. I hoped they would understand in time, especially if I re-established myself in the Reading team. Come the day of the game, as the team was announced, Dillon told me there had been a change and I was now a substitute. It was not my way to kick up a huge fuss and ask why they had persuaded me to stay instead of going home, but I was really upset that I was not picked to play for Reading when I could have played for Bermuda. As the game went on it seemed more and more likely I would be coming on, but as the clock ticked on nothing happened and I never came on at all.

That told me all I needed to know about my future with Reading, and I knew that I needed to leave. Increasingly I was thinking of my life after football and, at 35, I knew my time in the game was coming to an end. Much would depend on the next few months of the season as to whether I decided to call time earlier than planned.

It wasn't a totally bad month, though. After England beat South Africa in the 2003 Rugby World Cup in Australia, England's Will Greenwood said in an interview later that he'd scored his try after 'taking the old Shaun Goater touch', following Lewis Moody's charge-down! Will claimed his first touch was Goater-style before following it up and putting it in the net. I managed to get hold of his mobile number and sent him a text – 'Feed the Will and he will score!' I knew he was a City fan but didn't realise how highly he thought of me.

I got the chance to thank him personally after BBC Radio 5 Live's Brian Alexander arranged for me to link up live on his show shortly after England beat Australia to win the World Cup. Will was wandering the streets of Sydney as we spoke on his mobile, which was all a bit surreal. When Will later appeared on the Frank Skinner Show, he told him he'd had a text from me withing him luck before the game. He then added that Jonny

Wilkinson had been contacted by his mate David Beckham – 'Awesome,' said Will, 'Wilkinson gets Beckham, I get the real legend.' You can't ask for a better accolade than that, can you?

CHAPTER SEVENTEEN
Sent to Coventry

There were some things about Steve Coppell I thought he could perhaps handle better, but there was also a lot to admire. He is very non-confrontational and it is almost a case of 'my door is always open but don't come in', but his overall style of managing is how I believe I would do it if I were in the same position. The only difference would be that I would tell players what I wanted from them, whereas he does not. If you are substituted or dropped, he never explains why; you would go and ask him what his reasons were and he would give a vague answer without really going into detail. You need to know what the problem is; if you are dropped because you are doing something wrong, you need to know as early as possible so that you can do something about it. Some managers tell you, either privately or in front of everyone, but Coppell would just leave it completely. That is his style and you have to say it's been successful for him and Reading.

In my view, his main asset was his unique way of explaining how we could get at the opposition by exposing their weaknesses. He would watch a lot from the sidelines in training and observe players and their mentality, how their confidence was; but when he described other teams and what made them tick, then he really came into his own. His analysis was excellent and totally original, and I learned a lot from his methods. On one occasion we were preparing for an away game with Stoke and he said, 'When you see Ade Akinbiyi racing around and his dreads going all over the place, coupled with the passion and anger in his face, that typifies Stoke. If you can stop those dreads going from side to side and keep their fans from singing "Delilah", you're halfway there.' I will never forget Coppell's simple but intelligent way of out-smarting the opposition just by working out what really got them at it.

Sometimes I would look around the dressing room and wonder just how many of the lads understood what he was trying to say. Undoubtedly it went over the heads of a lot of them, but I thought that this guy was talking some very, very clever stuff. In that respect, Coppell was excellent, and it was only because of my experience in the game that I could tune into his wavelength. I used to love hearing his half-time talks and observations, because more often than not it was quite profound. Half-time chats in football are invariably the same old 'get stuck in his face!' and so on, but he was never like that.

The most disappointing thing of all was that Coppell did not recognise that I understood him perfectly, and perhaps the chance of a fruitful working relationship was missed – possibly because I had gone to see him in his first week at the club and given him the wrong impression. My thoughts on Nicky Forster were simply to benefit the team and Nicky, but it is entirely possible he thought I was a bit of a know-all and was sticking my nose in where it was not wanted. I felt I was doing the right thing at the time because it was a problem that I really believed could cost us promotion. Perhaps I should have let him see the problem for himself, but sometimes you have to speak up if you feel it is the right thing to do.

There were a lot of things to admire about Reading and it is a shame things went the way they did. They have a great chairman in John Madejski and I had a very good relationship with him. He also had his own unique way of doing things, one of which was to come down to the dressing room just before a match and give the lads a little speech. He would say things such as, 'It's a great opportunity today lads, we can go top if we win and we've got 18,000 fans out there, so go and do what you've been doing in the last three games'. Then he would shout, 'Come on!' and punch the air. The lads would clap and shout, 'Cheers, chairman!' and then he would leave. Everyone would turn and laugh, asking each other, 'What was all that about?' Coppell would just smile and say it was something the chairman had to do, but we were all singing from the same team sheet and we understood he was trying to motivate us. Everyone had a great respect for the chairman and we were all aware how much he had done for the club.

So far as I was concerned, by the second half of the 2004/5 campaign I had been pretty much frozen out of the team, and so I took the opportunity of a spare Saturday to travel to Manchester for the FA Cup fifth round tie between United and City. For years I had wanted to experience the City fans' passion and sit among them when they celebrated a goal. For years I had watched them go ballistic and wondered how it actually felt, and with things as they were at the Madejski Stadium I could not think of a better time to go. What an experience! It was a most amazing day. My friend Julie England, who had suggested the idea of attending a

Manchester derby, arranged the tickets and we met up to go to the game. I wore a hat in a meek effort to disguise myself but it did absolutely nothing for me, and as I walked across the mezzanine level inside the Scoreboard End a City fan shouted 'Goater!' I had been spotted before I had made it to my seat, and this guy definitely couldn't keep a secret. All heads turned, and hundreds of City fans broke out into a chorus of 'Feed the Goat'. The next thing, about 300 fans surrounded me and lifted me up shoulder high and started singing again. Great as it was, it was also slightly embarrassing. The stewards arrived and their first question was, 'Why didn't you tell us you were coming?' They told me they would have ushered me to my seat, but I explained that that was not what I wanted. I was there to experience what the City fans experienced when they watched a game and to be in the midst of them when they celebrated a goal.

I signed as many autographs as I could on the way to my seat and about four stewards sat around me, even though I told them I did not need any help. They were concerned that I would be mobbed and that fans sitting behind would not be able to see, which was fair enough.

I had been sitting down for about ten seconds and the word must have spread, because it seemed that every one of the 8,000 or so City fans knew I was there. They started singing 'Feed the Goat' again – it was wonderful. There were no problems and about 30 yards away Andy Morrison was standing and waving at me, so the fans chanted his name, too. Sadly it just was not City's day, and even though I was joining the fans in trying to suck the ball in, United went 3–0 up before City pulled it back to 4–2. I never sampled the wild celebrations, but I promised myself that I would return and try again in the future. It was good to be back among the City fans, and clearly nothing had changed with them since the day I left.

Back at Reading something was brewing in the media. I had made around forty-eight appearances, and as time went on there were suggestions that I was not being played because after fifty appearances Reading would have to pay City another £50,000 as part of the original agreement. I never believed that to be true, because that amount of money was not a problem to the likes of John Madejski and I do not think he would have been comfortable with the situation if it had merely been an exercise in saving money. I still had another year on my contract so there was no way they would have been able to drag things out that long. I did not talk to the press about it and the club said nothing either, until Coppell finally came out publicly and said that I was not being played because I was not part of his plans. I was happy with that, because at least it did not allow the impression that I was a bad apple who was not trying in training but happy enough picking up my wages each week. People wondered whether I had had some kind of bust-up with the manager, but the truth was I got along well with Coppell and nothing changed after he had made the declaration. We still exchanged pleasantries and shared the odd joke, only I now knew exactly where I stood, and I was fine with that.

City had got wind of the rumours about the £50,000 payment and that it might be causing me problems. Because I was in touch with the Academy a lot regarding fundraising events, Dennis Tueart asked if I wanted the club to remove the clause from the deal, but I explained it was not a financial problem – if it had been, I would have paid the money myself! Reading's director of football, Nick Hammond, began asking me what I had planned, and whether I was thinking of packing in the game. I told him that I just wanted to play football, adding, 'But you can't help me – only Coppell can help me'. By January I confirmed with the club that I was not going to retire and they said, 'Okay, well we need to sort something out because you obviously won't be playing and we need to bring this to a close'. Before I could do anything Micky Adams from Coventry City came in for me and took me to Highfield Road on loan for a month. This was the move my agent Mark had organised, being a Coventry fanatic. He knew I knew what it would mean to him if I did sign. He phoned me up and said, 'Shaun, this isn't a wind-up but how would you feel about coming to Coventry on loan?' I replied, 'I don't have a problem with that – I want to play some football!' He said he did not want me to say I would go just because he was a huge fan, and I told him not to worry, I would love to go. But there was one potential problem – and it involved Mark keeping his reputation among his friends. For years he had been telling his friends at Coventry, 'Shaun scored again today, lads', and so on, and it had been an ongoing thread. But what if Shaun Goater played for Coventry and did not produce the goods? It must have been heaven for him, because I knew he had wanted me to play for them for years, and I soon got to know the lads.

There were players like Steve Staunton, Stern John, Trevor Benjamin, Dele Adebola, Richard Shaw and my old pal from Reading, Ady Williams. It was very easy for me to settle in because the senior lads always stuck together and it was traditional for them to have digs at the younger lads. At Coventry, however, there was a lot of insecurity among the senior pros and they were all having little digs at each other. It was comical to be part of it. Most of the lads used to gang up on Adebola, telling him his clothes were minging, and they'd cut up his clothes and hang bits of them around the dressing room as well as leaving his trainers out on the pitch. Adebola thought it would be great if he had me as an ally, and tried to get me on his side straight away, but Staunton told me that it would absolutely kill Adebola if I sided with Trevor Benjamin and Stern John instead. Staunton asked me to do it just to wind up Dele, and I got into it straight away. I came in one day in a half-decent shirt and was absolutely slaughtered by the lads! I would wear something similar the next day and get the same reaction, and I was told that if the ladies who served dinner liked what you were wearing it was the rubber stamp that it was minging. I walked into the canteen one day and the ladies, all in their fifties and sixties, said, 'Ooh, that's a nice pretty shirt'. The lads duly ripped me apart. I had to carry it on because once you stop they've won.

I joined forces with Stern and Trevor and we gave Dele some terrible stick; he was still trying to get me on his side. We would hang his gear outside when somebody was being interviewed on TV and you could see bits of his stuff hanging outside the window. It reached the point when somebody messed with Trevor Benjamin's gear and he said, 'Right, that's it. I'm going to start cutting car tyres'. It was getting nasty. We were all senior guys and had seen it all before, but because nobody was sure who was siding with whom, in the end everyone came in wearing their gardening clothes. Poor Dele came in wearing stuff that was so old it was embarrassing, but he just said, 'Guys, if you want to cut this stuff up, be my guest – I won't miss a pair of eight-year-old jeans anyway'. It was old school pranks but it all contributed to a great team spirit, and ultimately it was that spirit that saved them from relegation.

The Friday training sessions were really competitive and that took me by surprise, because Friday was usually the last day you would want to go diving into a tackle or have someone steaming into you, in case you picked up a knock. In my first session we had a game – the oldies versus the young ones – and the oldies lost. The lads looked at me, saying, 'Well, we haven't lost in a while. We're not mentioning any names . . .' There was also the yellow bib, awarded for worst player from the game. The two teams would stand opposite each other and then vote who were the worst three players on the opposing team. I think they spared me because I was new. Michael Doyle won it once and was not too happy, and Ady Williams snapped when he was voted worst player. After that the oldies won every week.

The boys went on a great run of form. Unfortunately, Mark missed my debut in a crucial win over Brighton when my shirt was tugged in the box and we were awarded a penalty. Even though I was not match-fit due to the lack of a Reading reserve team I played four games in a row, which brought in 7 welcome points for the Sky Blues. Unfortunately, the chances were not falling for me, but I was pleased for the team as other strikers were scoring. I was on the bench for the last game of the season, a game we had to win to ensure we did not get relegated. To add a bit of fun, the assistant coach said that the last player onto the pitch celebrating after we scored a goal would have to pay £40, so every time we got near the goal I ran onto the pitch. The Coventry fans must have thought, 'God, the boys on the bench are really supportive – they're up every second'. As a striker, I could anticipate chances earlier than a defender perhaps, but I was up and down all game and you would have thought we couldn't raise a tenner between us. We scored six goals that day and the kit man lost £240 – he was last every time. It was a great day and there was a parade of legends before the game because it was the last game at Highfield Road. It was nice to be a part of such a special occasion.

I only played six games for them, but I knew my role from day one. Before my arrival the strikers could not buy a goal and Micky Adams knew he had problems because it was not just one or two, it was all his forwards that were drained of confidence. I helped out by doing some finishing sessions in training, but my main job was to help lift spirits and confidence. I think both I and

174

Trevor Benjamin, who had also recently arrived, did our bit and I reckon Adams, who had recently committed himself to the club for the foreseeable future, had the nucleus of a good team. I enjoyed my brief spell with Coventry; their fans were great and urged me to sign. I think they are going in the right direction, even though they probably had one or two too many older players at the time I was there.

I was still a Reading player, however, and they asked me again what my plans were, to see if I had had a change of heart. I knew they were hoping I would retire, because then they would not have to pay off my final year and could instead have offered me 20 per cent of any severance package they had in mind. But, just as with the club, my decision was not financial either – it was about playing football and about having at least one more good year. Funnily enough, my agent called to tell me that Southend had registered an interest, but I said 'No' straight off the bat. I had not finished with Reading yet and I did not want to give them the easy option of saying that another club wanted me. It was a couple of months before we agreed what my compensation would actually be. I still was not sure where I would be playing for my final year, but I could taste salt in the air . . .

CHAPTER EIGHTEEN

Thanks for the Cheers, the Privileges and the Adrenalin Rush

I returned for pre-season training at Reading, played in the first friendly and picked up a calf injury – the first of my career. I knew the club thought I was trying it on because there was a tour of Sweden coming up, but I told them I was injured and could not travel.

I was talking to people such as Kyle Lightbourne, David Bascome and my agent about the future and just trying to gauge what the general opinion was. The feedback I got was that if I wanted to keep playing, just do so. I did not want another season watching games from the stands and it was around this time that my old City teammate Spencer Prior called me and asked whether I would come to Southend for a year. He began to really sell the club to me. I said I would think about it and the chairman could call me if he wanted to. Soon afterwards the chairman, Ron Martin, began calling to try and persuade me to come to Roots Hall, telling me the club was going places and that the confidence that they'd had from the previous season would take Southend to promotion again. He thought I would be a good role-model for the other players and a great ambassador for Southend United. He also told me he had already spoken with my agent several times, which made me smile. Spencer kept calling too, and spoke highly of manager Steve Tilson and the squad, adding that they had just won promotion to League One and I would love it there, that I would be a great lift for everyone. The chairman called me again and asked whether I had made my mind up. I said I would call him in a few days with my decision. He called again in the evening and tried to sway me even more, and although I admitted that it did sound tempting I stuck to my guns and explained that I needed to look at a few things and would tell him after I had been away with my family for the weekend.

Shortly after that he called my agent again to see whether I had made a decision! This guy was not going to give up. I had to admire his persistence, and after a year of being surplus to requirements at Reading it was nice that a club was going hell-for-leather to get me to come and play football for them. Anita, the girls and I went away for the weekend to a nice hotel in Suffolk and Anita asked me what my thoughts were. I told her that I had planned to play another season at Reading and that I did not want to end my career just yet – I wanted to end up playing, so why not go to a club that were enthusiastic and seemed to be going places?

I knew Coventry were showing some interest too, but although they were higher profile, they had a lot of players in their mid-thirties; and I did not want to get into the kind of semi-retirement environment where the general attitude can be that if you are an older player and don't start, that is okay and not the end of the world. I wanted to be somewhere I was being pushed to the limit, so that each training session I would be worked but enjoy it because the young guys would be saying, 'Come on old man', and

I would be thinking, 'I'm no old man – who are you talking to? Some guy behind me?' I also thought that because everyone expected Southend to go straight back down it would be a great achievement if we could finish mid-table and prove people wrong, and that would be a tremendous way to finish my career.

Steve Tilson phoned and asked whether I had called the chairman yet. I told him I was pleased to say that I wanted to play for another year (they offered me a two-year deal, but one was enough for me) and I would love to join Southend. The reply came, 'Brilliant! When can you get down here?' I signed later that day.

The only reservation I had was the distance. Living in Wokingham in Berkshire meant that it would be about one hour forty-five minutes each way and I had always lived no more than twenty minutes from all my previous clubs. The first time I went down to have a look around the journey took me three hours! I thought, 'This can't be the journey! What have I let myself in for?' Both Mark and I had done a little research on the Internet about the squad and other details, and it all felt right. I had decided that it was my last year and I just wanted to enjoy it as best I could. I was unveiled at a press conference the next day, with the traditional photo holding a scarf. Part of my contract was that I had Mondays and Wednesdays off, so it was not as though I would be travelling every day and I was okay with that, and I didn't expect to play every match either. The days off were also to keep the risk of hamstring injuries down to a minimum. All that driving would put tension in my legs and increase the chance of picking up a twinge.

I missed the first game, because of the calf injury I had been carrying, but I felt fine to travel to Walsall for the next game, so long as I was on the bench. I was only fit enough to come on for the last ten minutes or so, but it felt good to be out there and after a few minutes a cross came in from the right. After shaking off the marker I made a good connection with the ball and watched it fly in. That made it 2–2, earned us a point and was the perfect start for me. I was gradually getting to know the lads. Luke Guttridge was a player who impressed me. I think he was in the lower leagues because of his size, but he has the attributes to be a really good player – he is tenacious, good on the ball, has a good shot with either foot, can pass the ball accurately over distance, and I think we will hear more of him in the future. When I first saw Kevin Maher I thought, 'What's he doing here?' Another good passer who is neat and tidy and seldom loses the ball, but he is someone who plays within himself. He doesn't hurt teams enough but is capable of doing much more; he reminded me of a Graham Kavanagh-type midfielder. Freddy Eastwood was a raw talent with good ability and awareness; he needs to improve his strength and score more goals inside the box because he scores from distance regularly, but his future is in the Premiership. Darryl Flahavan is a good goalkeeper, very consistent, but at 5ft 11in his size might be against him for a keeper. Adam Barrett impressed me because he was an honest, hard worker who gave his all every day and I think because of his endeavour alone he will go further. So with the work ethic and team spirit, plus a sprinkling of good players, I thought we would do reasonably well and were certainly good enough to stay up. On the pitch I had experience to share, and that would come in useful over the coming months. I knew my role would be more than just being a scoring striker; I expected to get maybe a dozen goals or so over the course of the season, and also help provide a number of assists. I would link play and lay off for others, and I supposed it was a kind of Teddy Sheringham role that I would try to play.

When I had first looked around Boots and Laces – Southend's training ground – I thought it a fairly decent facility with a number of pitches, and I had certainly seen a lot worse. What I had not realised was that the club did not own it and that it was open to the public in the afternoons! That surprised me, but it is what the lower league clubs have to do. At times it reminded me of my humble beginnings with North Village. Roots Hall left a lot to be desired, but it was the stability of the club that had attracted me, coupled with the management and the desire of the players. With a new stadium planned, everything was in place to move forward, and so what if the ground was old? It had character and it was our home, and we could make it difficult for teams to go there and win.

We played Colchester in a derby at Layer Road and I was respectful of what this game meant to Southend fans. It did not matter what league I played in, when it came to derby day I knew there was no game that matched up for both sets of fans. I had played for Rotherham against Chesterfield, the Bristol derby and the Manchester derby, and for the Southend and Colchester fans this game was as big as any of those – you try telling them their derby means less than City against United.

I seemed to have a knack of scoring in these games, and perhaps that is why I became popular at most of the clubs I played for. The two I scored against Colchester were typical Shaun Goater goals. The first was a peach of a run and a great strike, and the second was a good run and a shank of a strike! I saw the ball coming over my shoulder; I realised I was not shaped right to volley it but I carried on regardless and the ball hit just above my ankle and lobbed the goalkeeper perfectly for my second of the afternoon. I ran off as Ronaldinho might – interviews later, please ('Did you mean that?' 'Of course I meant it!'). People don't believe me when I tell them I have practised the art of the jammy finish. 'I've mastered volleying the ball off my shin', I would tell them, and there is nothing like a shot that bobbles three times and nestles in the back of the net. There is a knack to it, trust me.

I was on a good scoring run and the team were doing much better than anyone could have imagined. In October we travelled to Bristol City and I had a really warm feeling going back to Ashton Gate. I would have been happy to stay at Bristol, had Man City not come in for me. The club had understood my reasons for leaving and I was proved right. They are a great club and the Bristol fans gave me a good reception when I came out to warm up. I was glad, because I had had nothing but good times there. We played really well on the day and Freddy Eastwood scored a hat-trick. I came off towards the end and the Bristol fans gave me another wonderful ovation, even though they were 3–0 down, which I thought was superb.

It was turning out to be an enjoyable season and the Southend chairman told me he wanted me to stay for another season. At that stage I was open-minded about it. I was enjoying myself and scoring goals, but I was also finding the journey hard and was not so keen on travelling the distances for another year. I noticed that the guys I was up against were getting quicker and stronger, and you cannot fool people once you are out on the pitch. You can talk the talk, but you have to be able to walk the walk as well, and I did not want to reach the stage where I was talking but not walking. I had in mind that I would make my decision around Christmas. The dark mornings and the travelling were getting to me, and I knew I could not do it for another season.

Steve Tilson trained us hard and I think that my being off for a couple of days in the week made him train me even harder. In fact, if the gaffer had one flaw, it was that his sessions were extremely tough, and that meant the lads were too fatigued, except on very rare occasions, to do extras. Every club I had been at you did extras, whether it was finishing, passing or whatever. It helps you improve your game by concentrating on the things you know that you need to sharpen up on, and there were a number of younger players at the club who would definitely have benefited from extra training. I did mention it to the gaffer halfway through the season and he made one Friday a lighter session – but then forgot about it for the rest of the season and it was back to business as usual!

Like Coppell, Tilson has some qualities that I believe I would have if I were a manager. He is totally positive about things and if you are having a bad game he won't come in and say, 'What the hell are you doing?'; he will only focus on the two good things you did in the half and not the sixteen mistakes. Then he will talk about what the team are doing well and very seldom does he mention anything negative. In fact, the only time I can recall him mentioning our deficiencies was in the final game of the season against Bristol City. He said, 'You won't have a better chance to be champions of this league but you're playing like you want to throw it away – get out there and play the way you can.' It was the first time he had changed his way a little, because it was not his style. He was not particularly into tactics, but would highlight what the opposition was good at and those players who needed to be watched, but he would only do that for about five minutes – the secret of Southend's success is great team spirit, a tremendous work ethic, and the players' desire to win. Without taking anything away from the gaffer, sometimes all you need is motivational skills and to be good at man-management – and he was first class at both. I was waiting for Tilson to impart his great knowledge upon me, but his way was to build us up and make us believe we were the best players in the world. Thinking back, very few of the managers I had played under had imparted any advice that had dramatically changed my life or style of play. Pardew had been the only one to go into great detail about various aspects of play. Maybe all you need to crack it is a bit of luck and good man-management skills, because it is easy to coach a team that is winning.

On the pitch I was doing my best to help the lads through certain situations. There were a couple of games where we found ourselves 2–0 down and I kept saying, 'Stay in the game', because at that level you will always get chances. If, however, you throw in the towel at 2–0 and there are still thirty minutes to play, you could end up losing 4–0. I would try to drum into them that it did not matter if we were two down, the referee seemed to be against us and the fans were going crazy. All it took was a long punt upfield, a lucky deflection and you get a corner. If you score from that you are back in it and you can turn things completely around. That was as much part of my role as was scoring goals – using my experience, cajoling and making constructive comments. I suppose I was an extension of the gaffer, but I was only doing what I had done throughout my career.

Another thing about Tilson that I really liked was that he never said, 'You see how Shaun did that, Freddy? You should do that'. I really respected him for not saying things like that, because I am a believer that you are all in it together and it would have made me uncomfortable to have been placed on a pedestal. There was never any special treatment – apart from the extra days off!

We were at the front of the pack for most of the season and it was not until halfway through that I noticed our final game was against my former club Bristol City. I had originally wanted my last game to be a quiet occasion with no fanfares so that I could ease out of the back door and get on with my life, but it would be a special day and I began to think about it more and more as we entered the final weeks of the season.

Southend had proved everybody wrong so far and we had hit the top at the turn of the New Year and stayed there. Now we had to ensure that we did not fall at the last fence, so it was vital we kept our focus. The club approached me to ask whether I would mind if they made the last game a Bermuda theme. It seemed likely we would win promotion and I said that I was fine with it, so long as it did not take away from what the lads had achieved during the season. I did not want it to just be about me. Some of the lads had never won promotion before and it was important that they were not left feeling that day was all about Shaun Goater. I thought the club would just say, 'Bring your blow-up beach stuff, wear your shorts and let's call it Bermuda Bonanza'.

As the days went by, they began to ask me what was authentically Bermudian and I suggested seeing whether we could have Gombey dancers. I contacted the Bermuda Department of Tourism and said it was a great opportunity for them to get involved, because it would attract attention to Bermuda. I sent them an email and left it at that – if they wanted to help, fine, that was up to them.

My family started phoning and talking about my last game. They were excited at the prospect and were thinking this could be a great day. The only thing was, if it was a party for someone else I would make sure they had a great time, but if it was for me I would say, 'No, no, I don't want all that fuss'. But as the game grew closer I thought, 'Yeah, why not?' and I started to get into the idea of the Bermuda theme. A few companies back home jumped on board and paid for the Gombeys to come across. I thought that was brilliant because it could only complement a promotion party, if that was what it would turn out to be. It would be an incredible way to celebrate the day.

My agent called to tell me about different organisations that wanted to be involved and about various ideas. I just said, 'Mark, I can't get involved with any of this – I just need to think about football'. One of the things he did say, however, which made my ears prick up, was how great it would be if there were Manchester City fans present for my last game. That was Mark's idea, and we were both sure they would come. I thought that would be absolutely awesome. Mark spoke with Ron Martin at Southend and the club put aside around 300 tickets for City fans, which were made available over the Internet.

I had a presentation in Manchester for the club's Academy around that time, and everyone came up to me to say they were coming down – if that was anything to go by, 300 tickets would not be enough! It was incredible that they were coming down for my last game; it would make the day even more special for me and, hopefully, for everybody else.

But we still had games to play and win. My last career goal came away to MK Dons in a 2–1 defeat, and I'm happy to say it was a Shaun Goater special! A cross came in and the keeper positioned himself where he thought I was likely to place the ball. But as the ball landed at my feet I scuffed the shot into the ground and the ball bounced in the air about 10ft and into the opposite corner of the net – another clean strike, and what better way for me to score my last goal? Well, I did have a reputation to keep up, didn't I?

With six games to go we were at least assured of a play-off place, but as leaders we expected to go up. We had a few hiccups along the way, losing at home to Gillingham and Doncaster, but we came back from 2–0 down at Barnsley – because we kept in the game. That proved to be a pivotal point for us because the teams below were continually dropping points. I inadvertently set up a goal for Mark Gower in that game, because as the ball came across I measured it up and sent a volley in that hit my shin and went sideways to Mark, who side-footed the ball home – a perfect pass. I told Mark, 'Don't worry, son. I saw you all the way!' Brentford, Colchester and Huddersfield just couldn't string a run of results together and nobody was taking advantage of our slip-ups. We were actually playing better on our travels because we could sense the tension from our fans but, despite the relatively poor form on the run-in, we were edging closer and closer and by the time we played Swansea in our penultimate game we could win promotion with just a draw. There were so many permutations going into that game that even Bristol City, the form team, could possibly scrape into the play-offs despite having been at the bottom for most of the season, and it was not impossible that we could blow it and play them in the play-offs ourselves. Imagine that – a possibility that my last *three* games would be against Bristol City. For obvious reasons I hoped it would just be the one.

I was glad we were playing at Swansea rather than Roots Hall, because we were not handling our fans' anxiety at all well, but we started terribly against Swansea, who needed to win to guarantee their play-off spot. We soon went behind as they flew out of the blocks and Rory Fallon scored on nineteen minutes. I thought, 'There's no way we're throwing this away – I don't have the legs for the play-offs!' There were almost 20,000 watching in Swansea's Liberty Stadium – a fantastic ground – and we had around 2,500 fans of our own. We just had to stay in the game and not concede. Again I was doing everything I could to convince the lads to keep their heads up, and fortunately Freddy pulled us level nine minutes later. Fallon made it 2–1 for Swansea after another six minutes, and as we went into the second half it was vital that Freddy and I started winning more balls so that we could take the pressure off our defence.

Gradually we began to turn it around and I started to dominate their centre-half. I could see that the lad marking me knew I had him mentally, and this was a significant battle to win because we were creating chances. Finally, on sixty-three minutes, I flicked the ball on to Freddy who turned a couple of defenders inside out and pulled us level with a smart finish – his twenty-fourth of the season. I came off with about fifteen minutes to go. Lee Bradbury, sitting on the bench, said, 'The results aren't going our way'. I just thought, 'I don't want to hear this', because there was nothing I could do about it, sitting where I was! I did not really want to know until the end of the game, but as soon as Lee said that I got up like one of the coaches, screaming at the lads to keep going. Tilson was fine, because he knew it could only help. I was hoarse from shouting encouragement and then Lee came up and told me Hartlepool had equalised against Brentford in the ninetieth minute. As things stood, that meant we were going up. I was up again, and shouted to Wayne Gray to get back and help out – anything he could do to help out, because Swansea were piling on the pressure. Our fans must have heard the good news on their radios because they began jumping up and down. Then the whistle blew and I ran on, still unsure whether we were up or not. I shook hands with a few of their players and then legged it down to our fans, thinking, 'Well they can't all be wrong!' and joined in the celebrations.

We had won successive promotions and Southend United were proof that hard work and team spirit can pay dividends, because this team had been written off by most experts, with relegation the most likely outcome. That's experts for you, and I could not have been happier for the lads because they had got what they deserved. We enjoyed the moment and were soon on our way back to Essex, after a few stops at various Welsh pubs on the return journey to refill the bar, of course – although yours truly, as ever, stuck to the soft stuff. I learned that Bristol City hadn't made the play-offs and so their final game against us was academic. We, on the other hand, could secure the championship for definite if we won, so we still had one more big day to look forward to – and for me it was the biggest and would certainly be one of the best days of my career.

I always felt my last game for Manchester City had been spoiled by my allowing the emotion of the occasion get the better of me, so as I ran out for Southend against Bristol City I was determined not only to enjoy every minute of the day, but to perform well and go out with a bang. The main aim so far as I was concerned was to win the game and clinch the title – anything else that happened was a bonus.

It was a sell-out crowd of almost 12,000 and as I looked around the ground there were Bermuda flags dotted around and it was wonderful to see the home fans, Bristol City fans and – sitting between both sets – the Manchester City fans all together in one ground enjoying themselves. What more, as an individual, could I have wished for in my final game? The Gombey dancers were superb and there was most certainly a carnival atmosphere at Roots Hall that day; and the thing that pleased me most – there was not one ounce of trouble. I tried to keep my feelings in check, but as I ran towards the centre circle it really hit me that this was the last time I would experience this and see such vibrant colours in a crowd. The sun was even shining, the fans were celebrating in the stands and I could never have envisaged such a wonderful day for me and my family. I took a deep breath as I looked around and soaked it all in, and I kept telling myself, 'You've got to be strong, now'.

Anita and the girls were sitting between the Bristol and City fans, in among the Southend supporters, so they were ideally placed to sample the atmosphere. I almost scored with a header and Anita told me all three sets of fans seemed to be willing the ball into the net. It was also funny because the fans were all having the craic, too. When the Bristol fans started singing 'City! City!' the Manchester City fans replied, 'There's only one City!' It was light-hearted and added to the uniqueness of the occasion.

It was a perfect day, and when I was substituted with a few minutes to go the ovation was incredible. I applauded all sides of the ground and all three sets of fans, who had been magnificent, and that was it – I was officially retired. The score was still 0–0, and what better way to end the day than for my replacement, Wayne Gray, to run and score the winner with three minutes to go, sealing the championship.

I took my girls on the pitch afterwards as I walked around thanking the fans, all of whom I could not thank enough. The Bristol fans were magnificent. I signed a few autographs, shook a few hands and had my picture taken. But when I got to the Manchester City fans, the passion emanating from their area was unbelievable. I felt enveloped by warmth and love and it hit me like a force 9 gale. A couple of guys jumped over and hugged me and one of the lads picked me up off the ground, saying, 'We love you, thanks for everything, thanks for all the memories and how you are as a person'. I couldn't move, it was a proper bear hug, but the stewards knew I was fine with it. One City fan had come all the way from eastern Europe specially for the game. Two or three more City fans came on and I asked the stewards to make sure the girls got back safely to Anita, who was about 50 yards away. I spent a little more time with the City fans before continuing my walk to the Southend supporters. I felt a real affection from them, especially as I had only been with them for one season, and it was much appreciated. I know one thing was for sure – if I had had my last game at City, I would have come on to the field with everything and come off the pitch no better than a streaker!

I danced a little bit with the Gombey dancers before leaving the pitch and I enjoyed it, and for the last 20 yards or so the Southend fans hoisted me up until I reached the tunnel. The team then all went up to the directors' box and we all sang a few songs – although the lads told me my next career would not be as a singer, having heard my rendition of the 'Larv it' song from *Soccer AM*. The crowd started a version of 'Feed the Goat' and I joined in, even though I was told by the lads that I didn't even know the words to my own song! I think there were several important factors – call it fate – that helped make that day so special.

Firstly, Southend clinched the title; secondly, Bristol City had nothing to play for so their supporters had come to enjoy the day; thirdly, Manchester City were playing the following day, so the City fans could travel south without the worry of missing a game. I saw a lot of City shirts the following day on the open-top bus tour of Southend, ending up at the pier. I could not have written a better script if I had tried. Sure, it would have been nice to have scored – even a Shaun Goater clean strike via my backside would have sufficed. But I doubt it would have made the occasion any better, and I would not have changed a single thing from what was a perfect day.

CHAPTER NINETEEN

Cheeseburgers and Dirty Nappies – Adventures with the National Team

I was wondering where to place a chapter on my international career and even wondered whether it might be better to sprinkle my experiences throughout the book, but ultimately I thought it would be a nice way to round things off.

I represented my country quite a few times, starting with the Bermuda Under-18s. We had a trip out to Belize in Central America for a tournament with a lot of my former schoolmates – players such as Dean Minors, Clay Smith and David Bascome. The team was made up of guys who played for different clubs and schools, and because of the size of our island we all knew each other fairly well.

We had a really good time and it was one of the first times I got a taste of another country and its lifestyle. It did not take long to see it was a very poor country, the kids running around with no shoes on, kicking old footballs in dusty streets, and it made me appreciate what we had back home. They all seemed happy enough, however, and made us feel welcome. I enjoyed myself, wearing the No. 10 shirt during the tournament and attracting attention to myself with a few fancy moves and tricks that the spectators seemed to enjoy. We played the hosts and Guatemala and we gave a decent showing, but the hotels had bare brickwork inside and the mosquitoes had the run of the place. The heat was unbearable but it was a good experience for me to see how football was played in different countries and under varying conditions.

I played a few games for the Under-19s, too, although I never captained the team – that was mainly because when Bermuda play everybody is the captain, and if there was ever a dispute with the referee he would have all ten of us standing around him saying, 'Okay, you can tell us all now'. The captain was the person who tossed the coin and that was about it – nothing more than that.

There was another time we went away, this time with the Under-21s. Andrew Bascome was coaching us. At half-time he said to me, 'It's two minutes into the game and you're trying to dress and undress a player', which basically meant trying to turn somebody inside out and embarrass him. He continued, 'You do that after two minutes and now they know what your game's about and they figure out how to stop you. They kick you and you're jumping out of the way and therefore ineffective.' What he was saying, of course, was spot on, and it was an important lesson for me to learn. Not only that, but I was wearing the No. 10 shirt, traditionally the flair player's favoured number, so I might as well have had a neon sign above my head. Andrew said I was advertising myself too much to the opposition and that I should play within myself until I had a chance to hurt them and – wham! It all made perfect sense. My mentality was to try to make players look silly, and if I beat three players and lost the ball my attitude was, 'Yeah, but did you see those three guys I threw off?'

That was how we all were in Bermuda – we wanted to look good, use our skills and tricks, and it was actually holding us back. Andrew said, 'You're on the international stage now and these things need to be thought of – you can't bring attention to yourself like that any more because it makes it easy for the opposition.' I might have been one of the star players in that team, but his advice to keep discreet was as sound as any I had ever been given and it helped me to focus more and to progress. It proved more than useful, because when I went over to England the coaches used to tell me to 'stop all that flippy-flappy, tippy-tappy football and put the ball in the bloody net!' because I had moved from the fun side of the amateur game to the business end of the professional game. People's jobs were on the line and livelihoods were at risk and so, over the years, I understood the concept. Early in my career at United, after I had played a match, people would ask me what position I was playing in, and I would tell them I was a striker. 'How many goals did you score?' 'None, but I set three up.' 'None? And you're a striker?' Things were different in England and it was only the net result, so to speak, that people were interested in.

I saw a lot of different countries in my early days with Bermuda and few if any could match the standard of living back home. I knew that, by comparison, my life was good, privileged in fact. After we played Mexico there were thousands of kids swarming around the team coach, looking for anything to keep as a memento. We managed to give out a few pennants and they loved it – things like that stay with you. Even though by Bermudian standards I lived in the ghetto, compared to some of the areas we passed on our travels I lived a wealthy life.

I made my senior debut, aged 17, for my country as a substitute against Canada at PHC's ground and the crowd went absolutely crazy because I was coming on. There were perhaps 1,800 fans, which was a good crowd for a night game, and I ran on with no fear whatsoever and enjoyed every minute of it. If memory serves, I scored a goal, too.

Dennis Brown of Somerset Trojans played that day and he was one of our best centre-halves ever. It was good to play alongside players like that, and I just thought, 'Hey, I'm gonna show my people what I can do', and to a certain extent I did – and I liked the feeling of playing at a higher level. We did not get any caps or pennants for playing and I never heard of caps until I came to England. It is difficult to figure out my international record with any accuracy because there are virtually no records available. That's Bermuda for you – laid-back is not even in it!

Over the years we rarely played international matches during the English season and I tended to play most games during the summer break. Though I've no official records I'm told I played thirty-eight times for Bermuda, and scored thirty-three goals. That was when the majority of tournaments or World Cup qualifiers would be played, and there would be a cluster of six or seven matches within a short space of time. We have always been realistic about our chances of making the World Cup finals, but so long as we progress each time the qualifiers come around, we know we are on the right lines. In 1992 we went hell-for-leather in the qualifiers to make the finals in the USA. Being so close to home added an extra incentive. We had a good side, good sponsorship and everyone really got behind us. We were confident; both Kyle and I were professional and David Bascome was playing professional indoor soccer in America, and this was our best team since the days of Clyde Best. We played Haiti in front of 20,000 fans and it was hot! We were absolutely exhausted, but I scored to put us 1–0 up. I thought it had been disallowed because it literally silenced what had been a very noisy crowd. At the break I was sitting in the dressing room, absolutely knackered, but I needed to keep up my professional image and could not let the lads see me so drained because I was the one they looked to, and I was supposed to be the fittest. They handed out cool, wet towels and it kind of sizzled on my head, and while the coach Gary Darrell was talking I was thinking, 'I don't want to go back out there – I'm hurting'. People might think we would be used to the heat in Bermuda, but it rarely gets above 85 degrees, whereas this was nearer 100, and humid with it. The boys used to have a saying when we were up against it – 'Think of Nick'. It referred to Nick Jones, the guy who had come over to Manchester with me in 1989 when I signed for United and had put us through a gruelling pre-season session to get us ready for the qualifiers. During the game the lads were shouting, 'Think of Nick!' and I was thinking, 'I'm too tired to even think!' The heat was unbearable but when a bit of cloud cover came over the stadium it became a little cooler and we found our second wind and were able to hold on and win.

I scored a hat-trick against Antigua, who were a really poor team, and we won that game 4–1, but the games in Mexico were always tough and I cannot recall ever getting a result against them. We played Jamaica, El Salvador and Canada in the qualifiers; El Salvador were the best team in the group. They had the patient, slow build-ups typical of a South American football country, but when they got into dangerous areas they could hurt you. We played them in front of 48,000 people with armed guards around the stadium. It was hot again, with an intimidating atmosphere on and off the pitch. The fans threw bags of pee, dirty nappies and even the odd dead lizard at us, but there was a great atmosphere and it was the first really big crowd I had played in front of.

I was also getting physically stronger and I scored a typically English goal that day, towering over a defender to power a header home – I managed about three of those in my career! They had been playing us off the park and that made the score 4–1 in their favour, but I was pleased to score a goal against a nation who had a respectable World Cup history. We played Jamaica in Kingston, which was sort of a derby match for us, and we were battling away and holding out at 2–2 when our centre-back Neil Painter went to head it, threw his arm up in the air and gave away a penalty from which they scored what proved to be the winner. We were devastated, and sat down on the grass at the final whistle. Then Bob Marley came over the PA system and the lads seemed to lift, one or two saying, 'Hey, they're playing some tunes now', and there was I, thinking professionally and knowing we had come close to making some real progress, and I couldn't lift myself at all. I think we had gone as far as we could with that team and we had given it a good shout, and we were at least on a par with Jamaica at that time.

The problem was, we did not really move forward after that and played the same teams and got the same kind of results without causing the odd surprise here and there. The wake-up call came for me when Jamaica did well in our region and qualified for the 2002 World Cup. They may have a population of two or three million, and some decent players who turned out for them through their grandparents' or parents' background, but they still managed to do what most thought was all but impossible – so why not Bermuda? I have been in a side that beat Trinidad and Tobago, and they competed in the 2006 World Cup. The USA have done fantastically well in recent years and, being so close, perhaps that might wake us up too, and help us get our act together, because when I was in my early teens Bermuda were playing America and beating them comfortably. Everyone seemed to be moving on except us.

Because there was no professional environment back home nothing was changing, but I was playing in a professional league and while I was progressing and moving up the ladder it just was not happening in Bermuda. It didn't help when Canada played Northern Ireland recently and put in a decent showing. We have been on a par with the Canadians for a number of years, yet they are obviously moving on. In June 2006 we'd slipped to a world ranking of 161, one place below Namibia, one above Sierra Leone and six places behind perennial European whipping-boys San Marino, so we can improve, and under Kyle Lightbourne, I believe we will. At least the Bermuda cricket team finally made it to the World Cup in 2006, which is brilliant. My old mates from the Bermuda junior teams, Dean Minors and Clay Smith, will be playing in that and now the government has invested $11 million in the sport, the reward for doing so well. That leaves me thinking about what $1 million could do for junior football in Bermuda, if invested properly.

I always enjoyed my returns home to play for my country. In fact it was quite refreshing, after being among the high-pressure world of the Premiership, to go back and hear the boys still talking about the kind of things we used to when I was a kid and to join in the banter and generally have a good laugh. I never needed bringing down to earth, but if I had this would have been the perfect place to be grounded.

One of my biggest disappointments was in 2000 when we travelled to the British Virgin Islands and Clyde Best had taken over as Director of Football. I was greatly looking forward to working with Clyde because he was somebody who had paved the way for me years before and now he was back, involved with Bermuda. I was waiting for Clyde to come in and impart something from a coaching perspective but he just said, 'Go and be the way you are in England'. I had expected so much more. Maybe I had got it wrong and his role did not involve coaching. I had envisaged much more interaction on the coaching side, but that was about as much contact as I had from him. I had lost count of the number of strikers I had admired and expected so much from, but got so little back. This had happened right the way through my career – maybe I was just destined to do it my own way.

Preparing for the game with the British Virgin Islands evokes one of my favourite memories of my time with the national team and, for me, it pretty much sums up the attitude the team had, probably right up till Kyle took charge a couple of years ago. BVI's pitch was no more than a local park with a few people scattered around, and they rank even lower than us in the FIFA rankings. We sat down in a local eatery for a pre-match meal and the lads ordered cheeseburgers and french fries – thick, homemade cheeseburgers with the works – and I just smiled and took a picture of this lavish spread. The boys asked me why I was taking a picture. I just told them it was for posterity, and I had to smile. Coming from an environment where food was a crucial part of pre-match, I ordered pasta and the lady serving behind the counter said, 'You know how long it's gonna take me to cook some pasta? I've only got these hamburgers cooked!' I stuck to my guns and waited for the pasta. We beat them 4–1 and we had a man sent off after ten minutes; that's how poor they were, and if I had known how bad they were before we started I would have had a cheeseburger with the works, too! I loved it, and the great thing was that the lads were doing exactly what I used to do when I first started out. I used to have a burger before a game and I would say, 'Right, I'm prepared and ready'. There was an infectious innocence to the way we did things.

My last game was in 2003 when we played El Salvador, and it came at the time I was at Reading. We had all the pro players available, which almost never happened, and I was gutted because I picked up a calf strain after ten minutes. The atmosphere was so humid that I only managed to jog around gingerly. However, the pace of the game was not much faster so I stayed on for a while, but I couldn't sprint or apply pressure when I needed to. I lasted about 65 minutes before I had to hobble off and I couldn't play in the return game in Bermuda a week later. There were 5,000 fans packed into the national stadium for that match; we were so close to progressing to the next phase and the whole island was behind us, but not only was I out but Kyle was injured and David failed a late fitness test, so three of our most experienced players were missing for our biggest game in years. We were 1–0 down, and as I sat in the stands I could see that El Salvador, who did not seem to fancy a physical battle, were waiting for us to really go at them. I said to Kyle that we had to go down and speak to Kenny Thompson, the manager, because the lads did not seem to realise how close we were to having a positive outcome. We had to win the game and we had a player sent off, but I could sense El Salvador were vulnerable even then. We made no tactical changes and took no risks, and in the end we lost 2–1. The manager seemed happy at the outcome, whereas I felt he should have gone for it and risked a heavier defeat, but that's my experience and knowing how it would be handled in England.

Thompson's reign ended in 2004, when Kyle took over as national coach. He had just returned to Bermuda after retiring from the game in England and was the best person to take over. I thought it was a brilliant appointment. He also made a wise choice of assistant when he employed Paul Scope, who played semi-pro in England and is a smart businessman in Bermuda. Paul came to the table with no baggage and is free with his opinions. He had no connection with the BFA and offered his services free.

With Kyle in charge, I feel the professional attitude we needed is now in place and we can start moving forward. The only downside for him has been that the majority of his first seven matches have been against professional teams, so the results, on paper, have not looked that good. We played City's Academy two years on the trot and lost 6–0 and 7–1 and we have played Santos Under-18s and lost 2–1. We have also played New England Revolution and lost, but all credit to Kyle for not choosing an easy route into management. He could have arranged games with BVI, Jamaica or any number of other teams we would have stood a far better chance of winning against, and his record would have been a lot more respectable, but what is to be learned in games like that? He wanted to challenge the players, and that has to be admired. He just needs to hang in there.

There was a Southend tour in July 2006 in which I played 20 minutes for Bermuda and 20 minutes for Southend. I scored two goals for Southend and one for Bermuda and the result was Southend 3, Bermuda 2. A fitting end to my career!

At the time of writing I am contemplating playing in a tournament in October 2006 for Bermuda against teams such as BVI and St Vincent, both of whom have players in England in the lower leagues, so they are starting to improve. But the pace of those games will be such that I may well take part, and who knows? Maybe I'll have a cheeseburger for my pre-match meal . . .

CHAPTER TWENTY

The Next Chapter: Looking Forward

So what's next for Shaun Goater? Well, the future is bright and the future is professional. I have been working on a project that involves starting a professional team in Bermuda playing our games in the American A-League, which is the third division in the USA. At the time of writing we were waiting to hear whether we had been accepted by their authorities, and if we are we will kick off the season in April 2007.

The plan is that the team will be made up from the majority of the national team and will operate on a professional basis, similar to what you might find in League Two in England. There will be a few full-time players and the remainder will be on part-time salaries. I am really excited about it and will be linking up with Kyle and Paul Scope. This is what Bermuda needs, because it will give the kids something to strive for; our long-term goal is to compete in the MLS (Major League Soccer) in the States.

Teams in that division travel from New York to Vancouver and obviously the expenses become much higher, but then so is the standard of football, and our players will become that much better because of it. I would prefer the team to be just Bermudian players, but if we have to bring one or two across from England to raise the standard to the required level, so be it.

As things stand, the kids have nothing to strive for; the amateur clubs they play for are not run properly and kids train when they want. There are no role-models or mentors any more and the youths choose either girls, PlayStations or drugs. Very few have the guidance needed to avoid those routes, but they will be able to achieve some small status being professional players in Bermuda, and that excites me.

The project is going to be run by people who have played at the top level and we will use our experience and contacts to see it through. I will be dealing with the media, sponsors and the public face of the team. As a director I will try to put the right image forward and make sure the boys carry themselves correctly off the field, which is important if we are to have companies or individuals invest in the project. Kyle's role will be along similar lines, but involving more of the coaching side. The team will train every day and I am considering a role with the BFA (Bermuda Football Association) as a Youth Development Officer. Youth development would allow me to do a bit more with the pro team, whereas the director's role is a lot more hands-on and time-consuming. The two good things are being able to set up structures and plans for the regeneration of Bermudian football and knowing that this is a format that works in different countries, so that in five to eight years the youths who have come through the system with the right coaching will be able to move forward and we will be able to say, 'Yes, this kid is ready for League Two trials'. To be able to do all this with Kyle is a terrific bonus. If David Bascome could become involved at some stage it would be even better.

As for family life, nothing is more important to me than Anita and my girls. I will balance my new roles with quality time with them, and I am looking forward to living in Bermuda again. My girls have dual citizenship and although they tell us they are English, which they are, I am looking forward to them experiencing life in the place where I grew up. The plan is for them to return to England to go to university and, hopefully, play for Manchester City's Ladies' teams – feed the goats! We are keeping a home in England so the girls can use it at a later date and we can return for holidays. It will be great to catch up on lost time with my mum and sister, and perhaps get to know my dad properly and build a relationship with him too. His name, for the record, is Michael 'Sabie' Wade and he will always be welcome at our home when we have get-togethers. I want my girls to get to know him, too. They have already met him a few times. They call him 'papa', and because I look like him they took to him straight away. Anita says I have a similar nature to my dad, and I look forward to finding that out for myself. People tell me he is proud of my achievements and if he is, that's nice, too.

One incident that happened not long before I returned home to Bermuda pretty much sums up the way football fans in England seemed to see me. I went to a pub in London where they were showing a game between Chelsea and West Ham with my friend Paul Scope and a few other guys who were all Chelsea supporters. This was a rough pub – full of ardent Chelsea fans – but I didn't care because I wanted to watch the match. The whole pub was singing songs and after about five minutes one guy must have recognised me and within a few minutes a pub full of Chelsea fans started singing 'Feed the Goat and he will score!' I thought it was brilliant! They followed that with 'Blue Moon' and I couldn't believe it – what a tribute. I smiled and thanked them all – and these were hard-looking blokes – but they made me feel at home and very welcome. As I watched the game, a man of about 60 came over and said, 'I'll tell you what mate, that's what these guys think of you and we're mad Chelsea fans. A couple of years ago a black bloke wouldn't have walked in here because we'd have done you in but we've sung your song and you've got our respect.' That summed up how I've been treated in England. I had to earn that respect, but it felt really good to have it, and I'll never forget that day.

I shall miss England and the life I have led here, the adulation, privileges, challenges and adrenalin rushes – I shall miss it all. We plan to come back for two- or three-week stays because we have met some wonderful people over the last seventeen years and we would not want to allow that just to fade away. We will always maintain a connection with the country that allowed me to live my dreams. But I think I will be able to cope with relaxing beside the pool, a big smile on my face and a lit barbecue somewhere nearby. 'Where's those burgers? The Goat needs feeding!' The song will live on, trust me . . .